Better Homes and Gardens®

USING COLOR AND LIGHT

First Edition. Second Printing, 1986.
Library of Congress Catalog Card Number: 85-60585
ISBN: 0-696-02180-3

BETTER HOMES AND GARDENS® BOOKS

Editor: Gerald M. Knox
Art Director: Ernest Shelton
Managing Editor: David A. Kirchner
Copy and Production Editors: Marsha Jahns, Mary Helen Schiltz,
Carl Voss, David A. Walsh

Associate Art Directors: Linda Ford Vermie, Neoma Alt West,
Randall Yontz
Assistant Art Directors: Lynda Haupert, Harijs Priekulis,
Tom Wegner
Senior Graphic Designers: Mike Eagleton, Lyne Neymeyer,
Stan Sams
Graphic Designers: Mike Burns, Sally Cooper, Darla Whipple-Frain,
Jack Murphy, Brian Wignall, Kim Zarley

Vice President, Editorial Director: Doris Eby
Group Editorial Services Director: Duane L. Gregg .

Senior Vice President, General Manager: Fred Stines
Director of Publishing: Robert B. Nelson
Vice President, Retail Marketing: Jamie Martin
Vice President, Direct Marketing: Arthur Heydendael

All About Your House: Using Color and Light
Project Editor: James A. Hufnagel
Associate Editors: Leonore A. Levy, Willa Rosenblatt Speiser
Copy and Production Editor: Carl Voss
Building and Remodeling Editor: Joan McCloskey
Furnishings and Design Editor: Shirley Van Zante
Garden Editor: Douglas A. Jimerson
Money Management and Features Editor: Margaret Daly

Associate Art Director: Randall Yontz
Graphic Designer: Alisann Dixon
Electronic Text Processor: Donna Russell

Contributing Editors: Jill Abeloe Mead, Stephen Mead
Contributors: Karol Brookhouser, Denise L. Caringer,
Cathy Howard, Leonore A. Levy, Willa Speiser, David Walsh,
Michael Walsh

Special thanks to William Hopkins, Bill Hopkins, Jr.,
Babs Klein, Scott Little, John Mikovec, Willa Speiser,
Don Wipperman, and General Electric Corporation for their
valuable contributions to this book.

INTRODUCTION

Color and light, to paraphrase an old song, go together like a horse and carriage. Indeed, you can't have one without the other. These constant companions account for much of the appeal in a favorite painting, photograph, or room setting—yet for many of us, color and light and the relationship between them seem mysterious.

Using Color and Light takes away most of the mystery, and shows how you can put these magicians to work transforming your home. More than 100 photos—in full color, of course—show successful color and lighting schemes. In this book you'll learn in clear, simple language exactly what color and light are and how you can use them to solve problems, create special effects, and plan rooms that bedazzle the eye.

Color and light are essential decorating tools, and they present some important functional considerations as well. Exactly how much light do you need on a work surface? Which of the dozens of bulbs and tubes on the market are the most energy efficient and practical for your needs? What's the best way to highlight a painting, dramatize landscaping, or illuminate a conversation area? *Using Color and Light* answers all these questions, and goes on to explain the electrical specifics of improving the lighting in your home. There's even a chapter devoted to daylighting, and how you might be able to bring more natural light into your home.

We hope this book will help you see your home in a different light. If it does, you might be interested in other volumes in the **ALL ABOUT YOUR HOUSE** Library. This wide-ranging series of books, from the editors of *Better Homes and Gardens*®, delves into just about every aspect of decorating and improving a modern-day home.

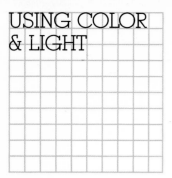

USING COLOR & LIGHT

CONTENTS

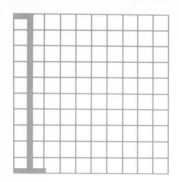

SURVEYING YOUR USE OF COLOR AND LIGHT

To some extent, most of us take color and light for granted. Daylight comes in through the windows under almost any circumstance, and walls can't help but surround us with color—carefully selected or otherwise. There's much more to color and light than accident and inevitability, though. Separately, and even more effectively together, these two elements can influence the decor throughout your home. Color and light have practical impact, too—consider safety, maintenance, and energy efficiency. This chapter raises a number of questions about how you think of color and light and how you use them in your home; then it introduces you to a variety of ways you could use them.

ARE YOU MAKING THE MOST OF COLOR AND LIGHT AT YOUR HOUSE?

When you look at your home room by room, there probably are features you'd like to overlook, and others that give you particular pleasure; there also may be features you think ought to be more interesting than they are. In each case, color could be the culprit—or the cure.

Think about which parts of your decorating plan seem to work best. Are there small items—a piece of art or an area rug, for example—that seem especially attractive? If so, could they be a more important part of your color scheme than they presently are? You may want to choose a hue from one of your favorite furnishings items and use it as an accent in the room, or emphasize your treasured piece with contrasting color.

Consider the possible impact of darker—or lighter—walls or a colorful area rug in place of neutral carpeting. And don't disregard a favorite color just because it isn't one you normally think of using in decorating. Purple may not be everyone's idea of a good room color, but a few touches of it could be a great success.

For an overview of what color is and what it can do, see Chapter 2—"Decorating with Color." It's difficult to separate color and light, of course, since neither can do without the other. For more about using both elements skillfully, see chapters 4 and 5—"Living with Color and Light" and "Rooms That Work."

Although color and light are united in many ways, lighting is less subjective than color because it has so much to do with safety and function. When you consider the lighting at your house, think about overall room lighting and about specific lighting needs for smaller areas and individual tasks.

Once you know how much and what kind of light you need for safety and convenience, turn your attention and enthusiasm to lighting as a decorative tool. Keep in mind the wide range of lighting fixtures and styles that have become increasingly available in the last few years.

And don't forget natural light. Think of sunshine—or the cool gray light of an overcast day—streaming through a newly added window. If that window overlooks a pretty view, all the better. If not, consider the benefits of a skylight or clerestory windows.

For an introduction to lighting, see chapters 6 and 7—"Planning Lighting" and "A Lighting Primer." For more about using natural light as a decorating as well as an energy-saving tool, see Chapter 8—"Daylighting."

A case study
The living room pictured *opposite* isn't terribly different from many others: It has two moderate-size windows flanking a traditional fireplace, the floors are polished hardwood, and the furnishings are comfortable, traditional, and neutral in color. Nevertheless, it goes beyond the ordinary.

The deep-toned ceiling is one reason. It's an important part of the color scheme, and relates well to both the dark floor and the base of the glass-topped coffee table.

The owners found innovative ways to light the room, too. To supplement the daylight coming through the half-shuttered windows, they selected unexpectedly contemporary uplights to flank the fireplace. Two low-key, contemporary floor lamps light the seating area.

CAN COLOR AFFECT YOUR EMOTIONS?

Black is sad, or sophisticated. Blue is calm. Yellow is cheerful. Red is dazzling. These are just a few of the familiar ways of describing color "feelings." Popular though these images are, however, they don't reflect all there is to say about color and emotion. Blue isn't always calm, after all: It also can be electrifying. And some shades of yellow are soft and subtle, hopeful rather than cheerful. What all this means, of course, is that color and emotion are closely connected, sometimes so closely that it's hard to say which comes first. Do you wear a bright color because you're happy, or to cheer yourself up on a day that you're not? When it comes to home furnishings, color is more permanent—all the more reason to be aware that the colors you select have a definite effect on the mood a room creates.

Mood isn't just a matter of happy or sad. It also can mean formal or family-oriented, active or restful, museum or modern. In different colors, the same furnishings can suggest very different moods.

Consider, for example, how the mood of the cream-on-white bedroom shown *opposite* would change if other colors entered the picture. Think of rich blue or bright yellow fabric at the windows, colorful carpeting and bedclothes to match, deep-toned walls punctuated by an equally strong-hued pilaster. Any of those elements would create an entirely different room in all but a physical sense.

The dramatic dining room featured *above* makes its decorative point in a very different way from the low-key bedroom. Here, the furnishings are no less simple, but the colors are bolder, distinguished, and definite without being brilliant.

Blue-gray walls provide a neutral background that's far from bland. Against that setting, the eclectically styled dining table and chairs, unified by a coat of black lacquer, stand out, adding both elegance and interest.

Because much of the color in the room is understated, there's room for more. A few accessories in complementary colors are enough to give the room, and its occupants, a new outlook. Notice here how various shades and assorted forms of pink—graceful gladioli, elegantly furled dinner napkins, and creatively matted artwork—add style and warmth.

For more about color and mood, see pages 28 and 39, as well as Chapter 4—"Living with Color and Light."

WHAT COLORS
SUIT YOU BEST?

In most cases, the colors that suit you best are the colors you like best. You should be able to find your favorites represented not only among wall coverings, fabrics, and accessories, but also in a range of styles and patterns to suit almost any decorating mood, from contemporary to country to traditional.

Once you've identified the colors you'd like to use, your next step is to decide how to use them. You could, for example, repeat one shade of blue in a kitchen, bedroom, and living room—the key difference is how much of the color you use and whether the items you use it for are focal points, backgrounds, or accessories. (See pages 88–91 for an example of a theme color that's used throughout a house.)

Not only can you use one color in many settings, you also can find many "right" colors for any one room. The two versions of one room pictured here illustrate that point. In both, the same earth-toned tweed sofa serves as both the main seating unit and focal point; both versions also have dark-finish woodwork and

polished wood furniture. What gives each version its own distinctive look is the difference in the walls—pale neutral in one room, warm rust in the other.

Largely as a result of this difference, the room pictured *at left* presents a traditional, rather dignified effect; the version shown *below* is less formal. Furnishings and accessories complete the subtle transformation—notice, for example, that in the rust-walled room woven-seat armchairs replace two upholstered wing chairs that match the sofa. In a similar vein, a collection of oriental accessories replaces several more traditional items that were used as accents in the room *at left*.

For more about choosing and using colors, see chapters 2, 3, 4, and 5.

WHERE DOES A COLOR SCHEME BEGIN?

When you decorate a room, you're more than likely to start with colors you like, colors you're comfortable with. Look at the clothes you wear, and you may well discover that you've collected an impressive assortment of blue sweaters or burgundy-striped ties over the years. The colors you stock your wardrobe with also may be the colors you choose to build at least some of your decorating schemes around. That doesn't mean starting with the walls, necessarily, or creating the scheme around your upholstery fabric. It simply means deciding what colors you want to establish in a given room, then finding a focal point and working up, out, and around from there.

One of the best ways to start developing a color scheme is to find an item you don't want to be without. Once that's done, you can choose other items to match it, highlight it, or complement it.

The neutral-plus-red bedroom pictured *at left* is a case in point. The walls, bedspread, and window treatment all feature gentle earth tones that could work with a number of colors in a variety of settings.

The homeowners allowed one of their favorite paintings to dictate the rest of what turned out to be a most successful scheme. The bright splash of red at the center of the painting is the key; there's not a lot of it, but it makes its presence felt.

The owners built on the first red accent by using several bright accessories in related tones. Note the progression from the pillow shams to the small print-patterned pillow to the upholstered seat of the chair near the window.

As you can see, where a color scheme stops is at least as important as where it starts. Too much red in the room shown here, for example, could have been overpowering; too little red, or too much of a neutral color, could have been bland. The idea is to find colors you like, and use one or more of them in amounts that make decorative sense in *your* setting.

To learn more about color's power, subtleties, and variety, see pages 24–36. For examples of successful color schemes, both familiar and innovative, in many different rooms and types of homes, see chapters 3, 4, and 5.

HOW CAN COLOR SOLVE DECORATING PROBLEMS?

Few are the rooms that don't have at least one visual shortcoming. Perhaps a window or door is in the wrong place, or maybe the room suffers from awkward proportions, a too-high ceiling, or cramped space. Confronted with problems such as these, you have two choices: Call in a contractor to move the window, knock out a wall or two, or perform other structural surgery—or "remodel" with color.

The cozy sitting area pictured *at left* is an example of how color can help turn a less-than-perfect room into one that's delightful. In this case the room had barely adequate dimensions and broken-up wall space; in addition, portions of the walls were in poor condition.

The room had several attractive architectural details that the owners decided to showcase. To highlight the carved fireplace and wainscoting, as well as visually expand the room's perimeter, they bleached and pickled the handsome woodwork to a creamy hue.

Then the owners turned their attention to the room's drawbacks. They covered the bumpy plaster walls with a patterned wallpaper that disguises most of the imperfections. For visual impact and rich color that wouldn't overwhelm the compact setting, they selected a soft blue as the dominant tone. It's dark enough to be interesting but light enough to avoid a harsh contrast with the near-white woodwork.

Rather than add a third color to the scheme and risk visually fragmenting the room's irregular surfaces, the owners created variety with pattern. One pattern is used for the wallpaper and the flounced sofa cushion. A related pattern adds to the charm of the upholstered seat to the left.

Color can do more than make small rooms look bigger, of course. It can lower extra-high ceilings, direct attention away from a room's less-attractive features, and help balance awkward proportions. If you'd like to see examples of how color (and light, too) can contribute to these and other improvements, turn to Chapter 3.

SURVEYING YOUR USE OF COLOR AND LIGHT

ARE YOU IN THE DARK ABOUT LIGHTING?

Getting the most out of lighting, both as a decorative tool and as a practical necessity, calls for some familiarity with lighting terms, lamp styles, and electrical requirements. Here and on the next six pages we'll introduce you to these subjects.

The golden-hued living room pictured *at left* has a great view, elegant furnishings, and a soft but unusually varied color scheme. Each of these features owes at least part of its impact to the room's creative lighting design.

The key here is an imaginative mix of lamps and fixtures. Notice, for example, the graceful table lamp to the left. Not only is it attractive in its own right, it also creates a cozy circle of light in one corner of the room. The sturdy floor lamp behind it has a similar effect in a slightly larger area; its spiraling electrical cord and three-tiered base add a sculptured presence to this segment of the room. Stage-lit plants and flowers that fill half of the panoramic window get their star quality from a very different sort of lighting. Here, three individual fixtures on a single track illuminate the carefully arranged tableau.

Effectively lit as this room is, it uses only a fraction of today's lighting possibilities, which are available in virtually all price ranges. For lessons about the basics of general, task, accent, and decorative lighting, see Chapter 6—"Planning Lighting." For more about your lighting options, see Chapter 7—"A Lighting Primer." And for information about the technical side of lighting, see Chapter 10—"Wiring and Switching Basics."

ARE YOU
A DAY OR
A NIGHT PERSON?

Some people like to get up early; others rarely see a sunrise. Some people never venture to bed until midnight has come and gone; others don't stay awake for even the first story on the post-prime-time news. Those are just a few of the ways that your inner clock makes itself known. Whether you're a day or a night person affects many aspects of your life, and your home should reflect your inclinations. If you spend many wide-awake nighttime hours at home, you need especially attractive and efficient artificial lighting. And if early morning is one of your favorite times, at least one or two rooms ought to have a color scheme that looks its best in the morning sun.

The dramatic living room shown *opposite* is attractive throughout the day, but has its greatest impact at night. Privacy and a certain self-contained quality are its hallmarks. Vertical blinds at the patio doors filter too-bright sun at midday and close completely at night. A color scheme dominated by gray upholstery and carpeting, pure white walls, and shiny black and dark-glass trimmings contributes to the sophisticated, evening-at-home ambience.

Equally important is the lighting. Recessed and track systems work together to highlight the owner's art collection. Strip lighting, placed beneath the low black shelf on the fireplace wall, provides an unexpected accent.

In contrast, the sunwashed room shown *at right* seems designed to serve as a setting for morning coffee or afternoon tea. Off-white walls, upholstery, and draperies are warmed by light that streams in through the French doors in the background. Rosy beige and gentle pastel patterns in the dhurrie rug in the foreground serve as further brighteners. Even at night, when it's illuminated by several attractive table and floor lamps (out of camera range), the room maintains its sunlit image.

If you'd like to adjust the color and lighting in your home to match your inner clock, you'll find more ideas and information in chapters 4, 6, and 7. If getting the most out of natural light is your goal, see Chapter 8—"Daylighting."

DO YOU KNOW YOUR LIGHTING OPTIONS?

There's a lot more to lighting than the incandescent lamp, as Thomas Edison's first light bulb originally was called. Now, electric light comes in a wide range of shapes, sizes, intensities, and hues. In any setting, both the kind of light—fluorescent or incandescent, warm or cool—and the kind of fixture the light emanates from have a tremendous impact. Whether you're planning lighting for a drab corner, a shadowy room, or an entire house, you have more options to choose from than you may realize. Here's a room that takes advantage of several.

The efficient home office pictured *at right* has more than space and well-thought-out furnishings to make it appealing: It's also virtually a showroom of contemporary lighting fixtures and techniques.

The owner, who's a professional designer, planned his work space with an emphasis on flexible, distinctive lighting. Instead of mounting a predictable fluorescent rectangle or a standard home-style globe on the ceiling, he selected a pair of track lighting systems. By adjusting the position of individual fixtures in each system, he can concentrate light exactly where he's working; by turning on all the fixtures, he can light the whole room.

Task and area lighting come from additional sources. Note, for example, the row of small spotlights installed below the lower bookshelf, and the small table lamp (in this case turned into a shelf lamp) that casts its light on the computer work area along the bookshelf wall.

This office isn't the only part of the owner/designer's home that reflects his interest in well-planned, contemporary lighting. For views of other rooms in the house, which was designed with special attention to the roles of both color and light, see pages 88–89.

Assessing your needs

Clearly, the lighting for this home office, attractive though it is, was designed with an eye toward efficiency rather than mood. A similar approach might be just right for your kitchen or workroom, but for a family room, living room, or bedroom, a different approach may well be in order.

Before you schedule a trip to a department store, home furnishings outlet, or lighting specialty shop, take a good look at the room or rooms you want to illuminate. Do you need lighting for the entire room, a particular area, or both? Does a single room provide the setting for a number of tasks, each requiring somewhat different light levels? Is one decorating style already decisively established? If so, do you want to carry it through to the lamps and fixtures, or would you prefer to introduce a new look?

The look you want as well as the purpose of the specific fixtures and lamps will determine your selections to some extent. If space is at a premium, for example, you may want to avoid floor or table lamps even in a very traditionally styled room; look instead to wall-mounted sconces or graceful chandeliers. If you want to use lamps themselves as decorative accessories, you'll want to keep them as visible as possible, which probably means you'll want to avoid ceiling fixtures and built-in sources, such as cornice or valance lighting; concentrate instead on floor and table models.

For more about planning lighting that will do what you want it to in each area of your home, see Chapter 6. To learn more about the types of lamps, fixtures, and bulbs that are available, see Chapter 7.

To find out how to make the most of the daylight that comes into your home, see Chapter 8. And if you'd like to try your hand at creating your own distinctive lamps or fixtures, see Chapter 9—"Lighting Projects."

HOW CAN LIGHTING ENHANCE COLOR?

In its own right, lighting is a potentially dramatic ingredient in just about any decorating scheme. So is color—all the more if you can see it clearly and without distortion. When you select lighting with attention to its effect on the impact and appearance of the colors in a room, you'll get an even greater return for your watts, lumens, and efforts.

oth of the rooms featured here have basically neutral color schemes, yet the overall ambience of each is quite different. The living room pictured *opposite* is a subtle symphony of earth tones with taupe walls, beige carpeting, and creamy-white upholstery. The bedroom shown *below,* awash in a soft pink glow, owes its color mood to pale salmon walls and bedclothes, dramatic black pillow shams, and glossy black storage units that flank the bed.

At least as significant as the color differences themselves is the lighting in each room. In the living room, daylight from two large windows (one of which is out of camera range to the left) is absorbed by the matte-textured walls, soft carpeting, and nubby upholstery. As a result, the daytime effect of the room is soft rather than brilliant, with gentle transitions from one color to another.

At night, when much of the illumination comes from adjustable track lights mounted parallel to the sofa, both attention and light turn to more reflective surfaces, such as the lacquered coffee table. The light bounces off these surfaces, emphasizing the contrast between the darker neutrals and the lighter ones.

The bedroom, too, gets gentle natural light through a large window, this one also out of camera range to the left. More significant in its effect on color, however, is the frame of subtle light that shines down from the ceiling, adding further warmth and softness to the room's pink-based walls and fabrics. Two high-style, high-intensity table lamps add drama, heightening the contrast between the pale walls and the dark furnishings.

For more about the interrelationship of color and light, see pages 28 and 29, as well as chapters 5 and 6.

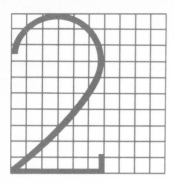

DECORATING WITH COLOR

Fire-engine red. Chocolate brown. Blue mood. Golden age. From objects and foods to feelings and ideas, color is linked with nearly every aspect of our lives. Because color speaks to us on so many levels, its power as a decorating tool is unrivaled. Colors communicate with each other, too. Some combinations interact boldly, others whisper subtly. Lighting and surface textures also add their distinctive voices. This chapter will help you orchestrate color schemes that will get your personal decorating message across.

WHAT IS COLOR?

Because we so often describe objects by their colors, it's sometimes hard to realize that, scientifically speaking, color is a property of reflected light, not a fixed quality of the objects we see. If you've ever bought fabric in a store, only to find its color looks completely different when you get it home, you've experienced the inextricable link between color and light.

Without light, we see nothing but blackness—the absence of all color. If you look at the color photographs in this book under dim indoor light or moonlight, they'll appear in black and white. Brighter levels of light stimulate the cones, the color receptors at the back of the eyes, allowing us to perceive colors.

Not only does light enable us to see color, light itself contains all the colors of the spectrum. Hold a prism to a window and it scatters light into a rainbow of colors, each hue produced by a different wavelength of light.

Sunlight itself is invisible, but when light hits objects, the objects' surfaces selectively absorb and reflect particular wavelengths. A red carpet, for example, looks red because its surface reflects red wavelengths to our eyes and absorbs the remaining wavelengths of the spectrum.

Color in the round
Although light passed through a prism appears in bars of colors, the colors of the spectrum often are represented on a color wheel, such as the stained-glass version pictured *opposite*.

• *The primary colors*, red, blue, and yellow, are spaced equidistantly around the circle. Primary colors "pop." Used together, they energize and activate a room. All the other colors of the wheel are derived from the three primaries.
• *The secondary colors* result from mixing equal parts of the primaries: orange (from red and yellow), green (from yellow and blue), and violet (from blue and red).
• *The tertiary colors* are created by mixing a primary color with its neighboring secondary color. Blue-green, yellow-green, yellow-orange, red-orange, red-purple, and blue-purple result.

Adjacent secondary and tertiary colors harmonize well and create what's called an *analogous color scheme.* A den done in sunny hues of orange, red-orange, and yellow-orange exemplifies such a scheme.
• *Complementary colors* are opposite or nearly opposite each other on the wheel. Complementary combinations such as red and green, yellow and violet, or orange and blue can be lively and assertive, but you need to keep them in check to avoid overpowering a room. Mix two complementary colors and they cancel each other out, creating gray.

The colors on the wheel all appear clear, bright, and pure—like the colors in a child's crayon box. On the following page you'll find out how subtler hues such as pastel pink, slate blue, and burnt umber fit into the scheme.

COLOR TERMS TO KNOW

HUE

SHADES

TINTS

Basic color names go only so far in classifying the myriad hues we can see. The sky, the ocean, and a policeman's uniform are all blue, but we need other terms to pinpoint the color variations between them.

• *Hue* is a synonym for color. The terms that follow help distinguish one hue from another.

• *Saturation,* also referred to as *intensity,* tells you how strong and pure a color is. Both mint and emerald are "green," but emerald has a higher saturation of the basic hue.

• *Value* describes how light or dark a hue is. White marks the brightest end of the scale, black the darkest.

• *Tints* are colors whose values are closest to white. When, for example, you add white to red and orange, the results are the pastel tints such as pink and peach.

• *Shades* are created when you add black to a hue. Navy and maroon fit into this category.

Shown *at right* are shades and tints that resulted from adding varying amounts of black or white to the blue paint in the large can. The paint in the small cans represents a light tint and a dark shade.

The importance of the terms presented here lies not in memorizing them, but in becoming sensitive to the nuances of color they describe.

Picture a white room with furnishings of high-intensity primary blue and red. Change the blue and red to pale tints, and you've transformed a vibrant color scheme into the soft pastel hues of a typical nursery. Or select a shade of red, such as brick, and combine it with a tint of blue for a country ambience.

COOL

WARM

2½"
63.5mm

FIRSTMATE

HOW LIGHT
AFFECTS COLOR

Color results from light waves reflected to our eyes, so the nature of the light source influences the colors we see. Theaters use batteries of different colored lights to create a multitude of special effects on stage. Home lighting is less elaborate and dramatic, but still contributes to our perception of the colors in a room.

Sunlight contains all the colors of the spectrum in roughly equal proportions, so when it shines in, it shows us all of a room's colors at their truest. In the photo *at top left* you see a kitchen and adjoining dining area as they appear in full daylight.

Artificial light sources don't precisely imitate daylight. Though they, too, produce all the colors of the spectrum, the proportion of the colors differs from sunlight.

• The familiar *incandescent light bulb,* for example, produces most of its light at the red end of the spectrum. Objects viewed under incandescent light take on a warm glow. Because the light source gives off a lot of red, orange, and yellow light, these colors are reflected to our eyes in greater proportions than blue, green, or violet wavelengths.

Compare the photo *at center left* with the one above it. Under incandescent light, the white kitchen cabinets and counters take on a yellowish cast and the blue of the teddy bear appears less vibrant. In the dining area, the wooden table and floor tiles take on a reddish tone.

• The standard *fluorescent lighting* used in many offices and stores produces most of its light in the green and yellow portions of the spectrum, and produces substantially less red light. As a result, this lighting has a much cooler look, and gives a slightly gray cast to red objects.

Although "cool-white" fluorescent lighting is still the most widely used, manufacturers also produce a variety of other fluorescent lamps. Warm-white versions add more red to the light's output to simulate the warmth of incandescent light. Other fluorescents are designed to approximate daylight as closely as possible.

The photo *at bottom left* shows fluorescent lighting in the kitchen and incandescent lighting in the dining area.

• *Halogen bulbs,* relative newcomers to the home lighting market, produce a very white light with little color distortion. (For more details about lighting options, see Chapter 7.)

In general, warm light sources work best when your aim is to create a cozy intimate setting, with a fairly low level of illumination. Warm sources are most flattering to skin tones, giving them a healthy, ruddy appearance.

Cooler light sources generate a brighter, crisper, more businesslike atmosphere, and you may prefer them for your home's work zones, such as kitchens and home offices.

If members of your household pursue tasks or hobbies that require very accurate color rendition, select a fluorescent lamp that approximates daylight or a halogen lamp for the work area.

When you select decorating materials such as paints, wall coverings, and fabrics, don't make your final choices in the store. Bring samples home so you can view them under the light of the particular room where they'll be used.

The interaction between artificial light and color becomes especially important in rooms that are used mostly at night, or in daytime rooms that receive little sun. A room that looks vibrant with sunshine streaming through the windows can appear washed-out under the reduced illumination of a few table lamps.

When you select colors for a room, consider *finish* along with color. Finish describes the physical surface of a color: flat or shiny, smooth or textured. Colors appear brighter and lighter on a smooth, reflective surface than on a heavily textured one. Even when the color itself tends to absorb light, surface finish makes a difference. Imagine, for example, the same spotlight shining on a black lacquer table and on a black shag rug.

A round-the-clock room

The living room pictured *at right* looks equally bright and inviting day or night. Floor-to-ceiling corner windows let in enough light to enhance any daytime color scheme. Because the designer wanted the room to have the same cheerful ambience at night, however, she carefully selected light, bright hues that maximize artificial light. At night, warm incandescent light enhances the room's gold tones.

White walls and ceilings reflect light and pick up subtle tones from the furnishings and carpet. To help you select paint for a white-walled room, many manufacturers offer a selection of different whites, some specifically designed to enhance warm hues, others intended to go with cool blues and greens. In this room, exciting color counterpoint comes from cool sherbet-pink polished cotton fabric that bounces light off the sofas.

DEVELOPING YOUR COLOR SENSE

Perhaps the key to developing a good color sense is to realize that color is fun. Look at the rainbow of furled construction paper pictured *below* and you'll probably be inspired to create your own symphony of colors. Experiment with a 64-color box of crayons, or a new box of children's watercolors. Let the array of colors spark your imagination: See what happens if you paint a toy chest an unexpected shade or buy a small accessory to add spark to a familiar setting.

Learning by looking
Discovery and experimentation are the beginning, but developing a color sense is really a two-part learning experience. First you have to get a sense of what works—an almost instinctive realization of how much of white it takes to cool down a collection of bright primaries, for example, or how much of a pale neutral background a room can tolerate before it gets bland. One way to do that is to take every opportunity to look at colors in both natural and indoor settings. (See the box opposite for suggestions.)

Then it's time to find the kinds of colors you're most comfortable with. That narrowing-down process isn't as specific as choosing a color scheme; nor is it as scientific as learning the definitions of hues and tints and so on. This isn't the time to choose exactly which colors you want to use. Instead, it's a matter of making friends with colors, deciding what types of colors (primaries, secondaries, neutrals, earth tones, and so forth) and combinations of colors you like best. For example, if you like rooms with a calm, quiet, and rather reserved air, neutrals or the more subtle pastels are probably the color groups in which you should concentrate your search for favorites.

Getting to know color
On the preceding six pages, you learned a number of color terms. You also saw that different types of light can alter colors. You'll see in the chapters that follow how color can help with specific decorating or architectural problems, and how well-chosen color can add extra charm to the best-designed settings, too.

When you're thinking about color, then, think about its role as a modeling tool. Consider its ability to expand a small room or warm up a large, somewhat impersonal one. Envision—and then find examples of—colors that relax you, colors you've always lived with, and colors you've been hesitant to try.

Picking colors for your house
Figure out what you want the colors in your home to accomplish and then picture a number of colors that could do that. If, for example, you have small rooms that open directly off each other, you may decide you'd like to use low-key colors to visually expand the space. But *which* low-key colors? Pale neutrals, soft pastels, or variations of white? It's important to know your options. The more colors you look at in swatches, in color charts, and in use, the better chance you have of finding precisely the "right" colors. The more colors you see, the better developed your color sense will be when you're ready to plan a color scheme.

SEEING COLORS EVERYWHERE

You're probably already familiar with a number of practical ways to choose a decorating style or color scheme: When you're planning such a project, you most likely take careful note of appealing rooms you've seen in magazines, at neighbors' homes, in department store model rooms, and so on. Developing your color sense calls for still wider-ranging observations, however. In fact, it's really a matter of looking at *everything* from the perspective of color.

Two of the most popular ways to view color are to collect the paint chips that are widely available in paint stores, and to look at the paintings in art galleries and museums.

Here are some examples of practical but somewhat unexpected things you might do to further develop your appreciation of color.

• Take a walk around your neighborhood. Look at the different shades of green. Well-watered lawns, new leaves, late-summer leaves— all are of varying intensities. See which ones you like best. Notice, too, how those greens look with other naturally occurring colors. Think, for example, of how the varying yellows and creams of daffodils stand out against dark green evergreen foliage. See how the colors of different flowers play off each other—a cluster of randomly planted zinnias, for example, usually is a dazzlingly colorful sight; a group of lilac bushes in full flower is a restful and subtle one.

Also get a sense of how nature's colors work with those that have been built into the landscape. See how the accent colors provided by flowers act as highlights against the generally neutral-color houses. Look at bricks—ideally of different ages—to get an idea of different reds and oranges, for example; look carefully at a home's fieldstone front, and you'll probably see a subtle mix of several closely related neutrals—grays, browns, and in-betweens.

• Go to your favorite fabric or needlework supply store. Look at the array of yarn. A well-arranged display of Persian yarn, for example, offers wonderful gradations within a color family—medium, light medium, dark medium, and so on. These are dyed for needlepoint projects calling for subtle shading, of course, but they're also an ideal tool for discovering how wide the range can be within a single color family. At the very least, this form of exploring probably will make you want to start a new bargello project; it also should be a good way to develop your color sense.

The same is true of fabrics. Look first at displays of solids—bolts of broadcloth, for example. They have relatively little texture, but often are quite intense in color. You will get an idea of what clean, uncomplicated colors look like without the distraction of pattern or complex texture, and you also may get some fresh ideas for combinations when you see the different bolts next to each other. Next look at the patterned fabrics. Keep your eyes open for patterns that catch your eye—the eye-catching feature may be an unexpected use of color, as well as an especially attractive shape or proportion in the pattern itself.

PLANNING A COLOR SCHEME

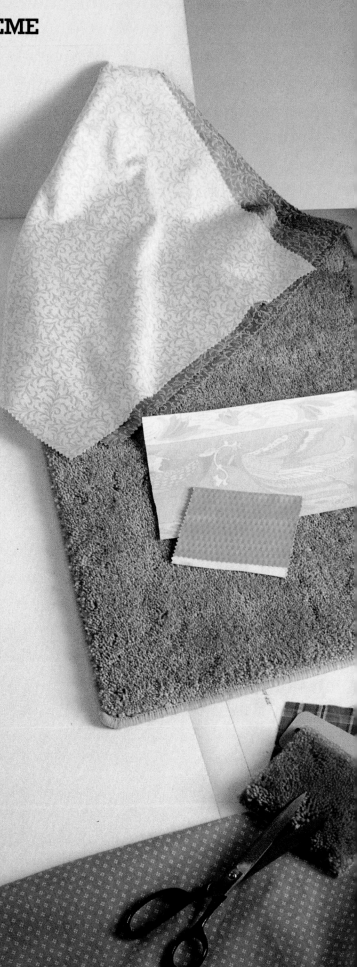

Whether you want to develop a color scheme for an entire house, or just for one or two rooms, now is the time to pick your favorite colors and plan how to use them. Before you get specific, however, here are a few general pointers to keep in mind.

• Even if you are only thinking about decorating one room at the moment, give some thought to how the new color scheme will work with the rest of the house. If the room in question is visible from other rooms, be sure that the view will be pleasing in both directions, with neither clashes nor monotony to spoil the effect.

• Collect samples of the colors you're considering—swatches and paint chips are made to be brought home and viewed in their future surroundings. Conversely, if you have an item you'd like to build a color scheme around, try to bring it—or a part of it—with you when you start your color search; it will help you narrow your choices. A selection of samples as varied and detailed as the one pictured here is the way to a perfectly coordinated scheme, whatever the colors.

• Pay some attention to familiar color scheme advice, but don't let it keep you from using the colors you like best. For example, warm colors make a north-facing room more cheerful, and cool colors create a restful setting in a study or bedroom. If the colors you like best don't meet these criteria, use them as accents.

Most important, remember that there's no one right color scheme for any room. The same room can be charming in any number of ways.

Types of color schemes
There are several types of color schemes. The type you use may determine whether the colors you select will enliven a setting, overpower it, highlight its good points, or help the negatives blend into the positives. In short, it's as much the type of color scheme you use as the colors themselves that makes a difference.

• *Monochromatic* schemes are based on a single hue, although not necessarily just one shade of that hue. Keep the need for variety in mind when you select a monochromatic color scheme. You'll need to use variations of the hue to keep the scheme interesting. Keep in mind, too, that differences in textures are very important to the success of this kind of scheme.

• *Analogous* color schemes also use closely related colors—in this case, colors that are adjacent to each other on the color wheel. This type of scheme provides more variety than monochromatic schemes; it usually incorporates between three and five hues (but only one primary color).

• *Complementary* color schemes use colors that are directly opposite each other on the color wheel. This is a bold use of color and usually works best if one of the colors is used in noticeably larger quantity than the other. You don't need to limit yourself to just two complementary hues, though: It's sometimes rewarding to devise a double complementary scheme using two adjacent hues and both their complements.

For more about the different types of color schemes and examples of each, see pages 34–37.

USING PRIMARY AND COMPLEMENTARY COLORS

As with a firm handshake, primary and complementary color combinations make strong first impressions. Even after you've been in rooms decorated with these color schemes for some time, the hues tend to assert their presence rather than fade into the background. In their purest "color-wheel" tones, primary and complementary combinations can overpower many spaces. Carefully balanced in value, however, these colors can be both dramatic and comfortable to live with.

When you begin to envision a color scheme, large unbroken blocks of different colors next to each other may come to mind first. Translate from the abstract into a working room scheme, though, and you'll find that a host of variations come into play. As you'll see from the groupings of sample swatches on these pages, color can be felt in a room with painted walls, but printed fabric can bring pattern and texture along with color. It's not only the colors you select but also the packages they come in that create the final look of a particular room. Use these groupings to help you start thinking about combining colors in real room settings.

The collection of swatches *at upper right* relies on a soft, yet vibrant, red to anchor the color scheme. Liberal doses of white help balance the strong reds. The compatible floral patterns bring in the other two primaries, blue and yellow, along with red's complement, green. Note, however, that with the exception of red, all the other hues are subdued versions of their base colors.

Though all of these samples coordinate with each other, the key to using them successfully in a room is the right distribution. If, for example, you chose the red carpet for a master bedroom, you probably would not want to cover the bed with the red-background print; the dominance of red would be overwhelming. Picture the same room with the white-background floral on the bed, and the other print as a window treatment or on a seating piece, and the effect is more balanced and pleasing.

The swatches *opposite, below* represent a sophisticated toned-down version of a red, yellow, and blue primary scheme. Yellow steps down to gold, blue to navy, and red to rose and salmon.

If you wish all mornings were sunny ones, think of waking up in a room colored with the gentle yellows shown *at upper right.* Here, primary yellow has been tinted and muted until it becomes almost a neutral. Mated with a cream-colored fabric, the selection of yellow patterns and solids would reflect light and cast a buttery glow throughout a room.

The color scheme illustrated *at lower right* cuts across the color wheel to connect complementary forest green and burnt orange. Two delicate floral mini-prints on white backgrounds inject a lighthearted note in counterpoint to the rich strong colors.

THE POWER
OF NEUTRALS

Bold color schemes demand our attention. Their strong hues act like magnets, immediately drawing the eye. Rooms dressed in neutrals engage us in a gentler way. The eye wanders over surfaces, shapes, and textures, getting acquainted with the space at a more leisurely pace.

Neutral color schemes are built around the ''un-colors''— black, white, gray, beige, and brown. You can mix and match neutrals, or select one family and explore its many variations.

The latter approach unites the grouping of samples *at upper right,* whose colors unfold from warm tan to pale cream. Soothing and undemanding, these colors expand space around you, letting you relax at the center. A monochromatic scheme such as this one relies on contrasts in texture, pattern, and value to generate visual interest.

Cool gray, in several variations, dominates the collection *at lower right.* Golden beige and cream were added to warm up the mix. Introducing soft melon hues personalizes the scheme and subtly raises the visual excitement level.

This approach illustrates one of the great advantages of a neutral scheme: versatility. Once you've set a neutral background you can alter the look of the entire space by simply adding or changing a few elements. Not sure whether a color that you love at the moment will wear well or grow tiresome over time? Try it out safely and inexpensively as an accent color in a primarily neutral room.

You can add an element of drama to a neutral scheme by increasing the degree of contrast between dark and light hues. Bring in the extremes on

the value scale, instead of re-
stricting your selections to the
middle range. In the scheme
shown *at upper right,* gray
gets darker and stronger until
it verges on black. Texture and
pattern become bolder too, in
strongly veined marble and
crisp white-and-charcoal
tweed. Here, instead of a pale
melon, rich salmon holds its
own against the deep grays.

A fail-safe color plan
No color clashes with white, so
you can feel secure combining
it with any hue. Lavish white
on walls, ceilings, and major
furniture pieces, then inject a
little zing with colorful accessories, or window and floor
treatments. You might prefer,
instead, to increase the proportion of color in a room and
let crisp white become the element of contrast. In the green-
and-white scheme pictured *at
lower right,* mini-print wall coverings with touches of green
bridge the gap between the
spring green samples and the
solid white tile.

   You can easily build an entire house plan around neutral
color schemes. It's much harder to conceive of a successful
strategy that employs bold col-
or combinations in every room.
For most of us, however, the
choice isn't one of either/or,
because neutrals make good
companions for brighter combinations and vice versa. For
example, you can lead the eye
in and out of a room full of
strong blues by using blue as
an accent color in an adjoining
neutral-tone space. On the other hand, you might want to use
a neutral floor covering
throughout the house and let
the colors of other items vary
from area to area.

SETTING
A MOOD
WITH COLOR
AND LIGHT

Dining rooms and the families who eat in them come in any number of sizes, styles, and personalities. The two pictured here are fairly close to each other in size, but the resemblance ends there. In each case, color and light play as large a part as the furnishings themselves in setting the mood.

The sophisticated post-Modern dining room shown *at right* is all smooth surfaces and interesting angles. The white walls and pristine quarry-tile floor create a bright, light setting. Subdued pink, used for the upholstery as well as around the picture niche and the recessed light cove above the dining table, adds an unexpectedly romantic note without detracting in the least from the room's overall sleek and contemporary air. Note how the two recessed fixtures in the background accent the artwork displayed along the rear wall. Further lighting dramatics come from the cove lighting, which is deliberately designed and positioned to give the effect of a loft-style skylight.

The more traditional dining room pictured *opposite* owes much of its charm to a good use of color. Here, dark green walls and a colorful folk-art rug provide a distinctive setting for the nostalgic marble-and-metal ice-cream set. This room gets most of its use at night, so lighting that emphasizes the rich color scheme is especially important. A floor-based uplight brightens the corner and the torchère provides general illumination with style.

CREATING SPECIAL EFFECTS WITH COLOR AND LIGHT

Tinted lights and *trompe l'oeil* designs may be the first devices that come to mind when you think of creating special effects with color and light. But for lower-key drama that fits smoothly into everyday life—and decorating—you might want to keep other techniques in mind.

The double doorway pictured *above* shows how successful a relatively restrained use of color-as-graphic-art can be. Here, the closer arch is painted a warm cocoa; the one beyond is a soft *café au lait.* Considered as a single visual unit viewed from the din-

ing room, the doorways make an elegant frame for the color-coordinated living room across the hall. And viewed as a series of smaller individual features, the arches take on considerable elegance as a result of their creative coloring.

Incidentally, although paint was used to create the special effect shown here, you can use other materials. Tape, for example, comes in a wide range of colors and widths, and lends itself to angular designs. Artfully applied wall coverings that show up well against the overall background

present another way to create unusual color and light effects.

The photograph *at right* shows a closer view of the living room pictured *above.* Here, you can see not only how the use of subtle color variations helps create a distinctive envelope for the room but also how light creates art. That's because the daylight that enters from the large window to the left and the smaller window behind the palm does more than brighten the room. It works with the spiky palm leaves to create constantly changing shadow patterns on the white walls and ceiling.

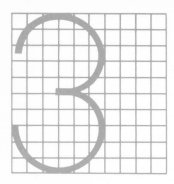

USING COLOR AND LIGHT TO SOLVE DECORATING PROBLEMS

Although the actual sizes and shapes of your rooms are constants, you can change their apparent lengths, widths, and heights by using color and light creatively. You'll never transform a tiny alcove into a ballroom, but you can, with just a handful of decorating ploys, put color and light to work in almost magical ways. This chapter introduces you to nearly a dozen problem-solving strategies.

SQUARE UP A LONG, NARROW ROOM

Awkward spaces, like ugly ducklings, can turn into beauties. And for problem spaces, there's no better cosmetic than color. Before you dip into a paint can, though, it's important to identify what the problem really is.

First analyze the room's surfaces. Most of the time you'll be dealing with a basic set of six planes—four walls, a floor, and a ceiling. The color you choose for each or all of them will make the surfaces appear to advance or recede, to be more important or less so in relation to the others, or even to disappear.

Next, identify other objects within the room that also contribute to the area's color balance. In most cases, these secondary parts will consist of window treatments, large upholstered pieces, small chairs, paintings, and accessories, in order of descending importance. Although none of these will greatly alter the apparent shape or size of a room, they can add to the effect created by a color treatment on the walls, ceiling, and floor.

The handsomely detailed dining room pictured *opposite* is a case in point. Elegant as it is, it's not quite as well-proportioned as it looks; rather, it's a bit long and narrow. To draw the eye away from this feature, the homeowners chose a bold wall color. Dramatic fabric, used for side draperies and cornices at the windows, helps to further divert attention from the architecture. The colors in the window treatment echo those in the Oriental rug.

Choose color for effect

Once you've identified the main and secondary features, you can decide what effect you want to create. Often, the way you choose to treat the walls provides the solution to the proportion problem.

In general, strong colors visually close a space in. Red, orange, and bright yellow jump out to meet the eye; they are called advancing colors. Green, blue, and violet are more relaxing to the eye and give the impression of receding. A dark color will have a diminishing effect on an area.

A long, narrow room creates a combination of challenges. To square up the space, you want some walls to advance, others to recede. Painting walls contrasting advancing and receding colors, however, may result in a room that just looks confused.

Often the best solution is a compromise. For example, if the wall opposite the doorway is the one you want to visually bring forward, and the walls on either side of the doorway need to be pushed back, use a strong, warm color, like dark pumpkin, for the advancing wall, and a soft white or pastel hue, like peach, for the other walls. The combination will even out the dimensions of the room and the tones will complement rather than clash.

EXPAND A SMALL ROOM

When space is limited and you want to make it look expansive, the old dictum, "White and neutrals will make a small room seem larger," is a good basic to know. But this doesn't mean you have to live without strong colors. One trick is to start out with white, then add color. The photographs here show how this approach resulted in distinctly different effects.

Almost any neutral, medium-tone color used on walls can help create a more spacious look. And if you unify with color—for example, by using the same color on the walls and ceiling and at the windows—you'll stretch space visually.

The small-but-proud living room pictured *opposite* shows just how successfully white and neutrals can be used to create an airy look in a room with modest dimensions. Here, smooth white walls and ceilings unify the living room and stairway hall, adding an extra few feet, visually at least, to one side of the room and

maximizing the overall sense of space. White shutters at two small windows soften the look without taking up space or interrupting the sleek styling.

To add interest to the smooth surfaces and understated decor, the owners selected a bright-red sofa and an equally vibrant poster to punctuate the fireplace wall. A shaggy, neutral area rug covers most of the living room floor, pulls the various elements together, and adds warmth to the space without overwhelming it.

Big, bold colors
This doesn't mean that deep,

saturated colors are off limits in a small room, however. The modest-size living room pictured *below,* for example, has a snappy red and green color scheme. It works because it uses darker shades of the colors, rather than bright hues, and balances the strong colors with neutrals.

A pair of burgundy-covered love seats and a forest green rug establish the room's color focus. The mirrored fireplace wall and a gallery wall provide the neutral relief. The mirrored wall also acts as a space-expanding tool doubling the room's apparent size.

COZY UP A TOO-LARGE SPACE

Have you ever visited a home with a tennis-court-size living room that sits empty in all its grandeur, while a small den or family room brims with activity? If this happens to be a problem at your house, perhaps it's time to call on color for help. A deft use of room-shrinking colors can give your too-large room needed warmth and intimacy, and help you break up its space into smaller, more inviting activity and conversation areas.

Choosing a color scheme that's instantly warm and inviting is the most likely first step in tightening up a too-large space. For example, just as an airy light-on-light theme can open up an overly snug den, a rich combination of darker or warmer colors, like the deep red and soft pinks pictured *at right,* can help create a more livable atmosphere in an oversize room.

Start with the background
The largest areas in a room—the walls, floor, and ceiling—are where the most color impact can be achieved. For example, using a deep raspberry red for the carpet in this super-spacious bedroom sets an unexpectedly cozy mood.

The miniprint upholstery on the armchairs picks up both the carpet color and the muted pinks used elsewhere in the room; the pink and white print used for the bedspread and roller shades carries the color scheme to all corners of the room. Using color at the windows is an excellent way to bring a room down to size.

How texture affects color
It's not just the colors you use that determine their effect on a room; the way you use the colors and the fabrics you choose are important, too. Two identically colored objects can appear to be slightly different in hue, for example, if they have contrasting textures. Rough surfaces—carpeting and some upholstery fabrics, for example—generally appear darker because of the great amount of light they absorb. Smooth surfaces, on the other hand, reflect light and so appear to be slightly lighter than they really are.

CHANGE A
CEILING'S HEIGHT

Short of installing a dropped ceiling or breaking through to the floor above, there's not much you can do about the physical height of a ceiling. But you can visually raise or lower a ceiling depending on how you choose to paint it. Here's some advice that can help you crown a room with just the right color.

If you want to raise a ceiling in a small room, your best bet is to unite the ceiling with the walls. And the best way to do that is with color. For example, the living room shown *opposite* really isn't large. But it has a spacious, airy feeling, thanks in large part to the homeowner's decision to use a creamy-white tone all the way from the baseboards up to and onto the ceiling. Windows and furnishings decked out in the same color add to the peaceful, easy-on-the-eyes scheme.

The space-expanding effect is further heightened with portable can lights placed on either side of the fireplace. By bouncing light off the walls and ceiling, the lights work to visually push back the room's perimeters.

Don't automatically assume that a low ceiling must be white. Depending on the other colors in a room, you might choose a soft pastel hue to help the ceiling recede.

Bring a ceiling into focus
For the opposite effect—to drop a ceiling that's visually out of reach—pursue the opposite tactic. Instead of colors that recede, select those that advance.

In the room pictured *at right,* painting the ceiling a dark brown brings it down into the line of vision, making the room look and feel warmer and more friendly. You might even carry the effect a step further by bringing the dark color down from the ceiling, onto the walls as far as a picture molding or some other natural line of demarcation. This is an especially useful device in older homes with very high ceilings and an abundance of moldings, cornices, and other architectural details.

CAMOUFLAGE
ARCHITECTURAL
DEFECTS

It's clear from the preceding pages of this chapter—as well as from your own experience—that not every room is perfectly proportioned with dimensions that precisely match your needs. Some rooms are less perfect than others, however, and some are downright awkward. If that's the case at your house, consider using color to help solve the problem.

The living room pictured *at left* boasts such an abundance of furnishings and colors that its architecture takes a back seat to the decor. And that's exactly what the designer had in mind.

As you can see from the view out the window, this room is part of an apartment in a big-city high-rise. You also can see that this room, like many others in similar buildings and recent-vintage one-family homes, has few architectural details. Instead of fluted molding, rustic beams, and high ceilings, it has smooth walls and ceilings punctuated by boxlike projections.

To add distinction to the room's unadorned planes and unexceptional layout, the designer selected a strong, rich color—in this case deep grayed-green—for the walls. Painting the ceiling (but not the crown molding) near-white and bleaching the parquet floor to a similar hue kept the dark walls from overwhelming the space and helped open up the room. Thanks to the contrasts between the horizontal and vertical planes, the room's effect is sparse and elegant rather than bland and boxy.

Because the room is so well-designed and color so deliberately used, there's still another architectural flaw that doesn't show. That's the odd-size and undecorative metal window frame that in its natural state detracted from both the cityscape and the roomscape. To minimize the frame's aesthetic impact, the designer chose to paint it the same deep color as the walls. As a result, the frame blends smoothly into the adjoining walls. An almond-colored matchstick blind echoes the floor and ceiling colors, providing an attractive accent along the window wall.

USING COLOR AND LIGHT TO SOLVE DECORATING PROBLEMS

ACCENT SPECIAL FEATURES

One of the real arts of decorating is being able to lead the eye to a room's "beauty marks." The degree to which a feature contrasts with its surroundings largely determines how noticeable it is. Consequently, the contrast you create with color and light has almost everything to do with how successfully you show off a room's special features.

Using color and light to make an interesting architectural or other special feature stand out in a room calls for some careful planning.

First decide whether you want to single out an object or area of interest, or simply highlight it. If you single out a feature, you'll bring the eye to rest. Highlighting it, on the other hand, attracts the eye but also keeps it moving. For the greatest impact, use color and light boldly; for a more subtle effect, try a softer treatment.

In the airy sun-room pictured *at right,* a series of French doors, punctuated by pilasters, gives the space its architectural personality. Inspired by them, the designer chose a dhurrie rug that repeats the windows' grid pattern, then picked up colors from the rug to highlight the architecture.

The doors and pilasters were painted white; vertical bands of yellow frame each pilaster, emphasizing its three-dimensional quality. Above the doors, a coral-color strip repeats yet another of the rug's hues.

Singling out a special feature

Fireplaces or interesting built-ins also are fair game for architectural accenting. Because these are small enough to be taken in at a single glance, you can choose to either highlight them, or single them out with sharper contrast. A richly carved fireplace, for example, might be painted or stained to stand out from the wall around it. Lighting offers another way to call attention to the features you want to single out. A spotlight or row of track fixtures could be adjusted to focus on the item you'd like to accent.

CARRY COLOR FROM ROOM TO ROOM

In all but very large homes, switching colors and color schemes from room to room can create a chaotic, chopped-up feeling. On the other hand, using the same colors in every room can be downright boring. Deciding when you should and shouldn't use the same color in two different rooms depends partly on whether you can clearly see one room from another, and partly on the function the spaces perform. Sometimes you want two areas to serve as one. In other instances, you might prefer that related rooms stay that way—as members of the same family, but not identical twins. Here are some guidelines about when and how to carry a color from one room to another.

The visual relationship between adjoining rooms can be vital, or just a matter of subtle harmony. If you want the areas to seem of a piece, choose identical color schemes. For example, the living/dining room shown *at left* was once two separate rooms. An arch in the center of the wall between them let you clearly see the dining table from the living room and front door. The owners liked the idea of an integrated living/dining area, but wanted more mealtime privacy.

The solution was to remove the original wall and construct a partition where the arch was located. Now the table hides behind the new wall; a slate-blue-and-white paint scheme unifies the rooms' walls and ceilings.

If you want to separate adjoining spaces with color, there are several different ways to go. One is to single out an accent color in one room and play it up in another. Or work within the same color family, but change the tonal value of the hues. For example, you might select pale blue for a living room and a deeper shade of the same blue for the dining room.

Keep in mind that you may want to use different types of lighting in the different spaces whose color schemes you hope to tie together. If so, realize that the wrong mix of incandescent and fluorescent light can set a beautiful scheme askew at the flip of a switch or two. In general, incandescent light accentuates warm hues, such as yellow, orange, and red, and dulls blue and violet. Fluorescent light, unless modified for red-rendition, enlivens green, blue, and violet hues and washes out red, yellow, and orange.

LET A LITTLE COLOR GO A LONG WAY

Color can be a great deceiver. You're probably already using such familiar techniques as painting uneven surfaces a dark color so they'll fade into the background, or coating a low ceiling with a subtle, receding hue to "raise" it. But where space or opportunities are limited, you don't always have a whole wall, ceiling, or row of windows to work with. A little color in the right place can make a big difference.

If you're trying to think of a way to brighten a space that doesn't really need any major revision, consider adding a touch of color. A bright color in a corner where you don't expect to see it, or a color that unexpectedly picks up an accent from elsewhere in a room may be just the solution you need to spark up a not-quite-good-enough setting.

The kitchen cabinets featured *at left* show just how well this can work. They're vital storage elements in a well-planned kitchen, but there's something unusual about them. The catalyst: They were installed without wood backing, to allow a vibrant blue miniprint wall covering to show through.

Thanks to this seemingly minor innovation, the whole work zone changes gears, going from functional neutrality to country-style warmth. By allowing the wall covering used above the kitchen cabinets to continue down the wall and show through behind the cabinets, the homeowners did more than add a color note to the work area. They also created a graceful transitional frame to an elegantly simple dining room adjoining the kitchen.

As this photograph shows, a kitchen, because its main components are often *not* strongly colored, lends itself especially well to this kind of color seasoning. Virtually any room that's dominated by neutrals, however, could benefit the same way. Whether your room gets its new color vitality from a few striking throw pillows, a dramatic area rug, or just one wall covered with a distinctive print, you may be pleasantly surprised at how far just a little color can go to add drama and interest to your home.

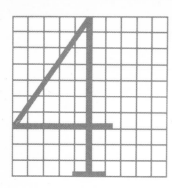

LIVING WITH COLOR AND LIGHT

The very words "color" and "light" suggest good things about a house. But deciding which colors and how much light isn't quite as free-form a task as it might seem. You have to determine not only the colors you'd like to live with, but also the colors that suit the size, shape, style, and overall "feel" of your home. As for light, you need to calculate how much natural light you can count on for each room, and what types of artificial light you'll require for convenience, safety, and, of course, appearance. This chapter shows how nine homeowners used a wide range of color and light options to maximize the livability and good looks of their homes.

USING DAYLIGHT TO ENHANCE INTERIOR COLORS

The sunlit, flower-bright corner pictured *at right* sets the mood as well as the color scheme for an entire room. Thanks to a generous allotment of window space—a bay complete with a window seat *plus* a pair of windows on the side wall—there's lots of natural light throughout the room at all times of day.

To take advantage of the almost porchlike effect, the homeowners selected soft colors. Fabrics featuring grown-up shades of pink and walls painted a subtle beige enhance the room's natural light. Even at night and on cloudy days, the room's light, airy charm is apparent, thanks to the well-chosen colors and carefully placed floor lamps that cast their light on the pale-hued walls and reflect it back into the room.

Pink-and-white mini-plaid upholstery fabric is the key mood-setter; the ribbon-print fabric of the balloon shades repeats the pink without making it an overwhelming presence in the room. Those balloon shades, in fact, are an especially good idea in this corner: They're translucent enough to let sunlight filter through during the day, but woven closely enough to be opaque at night and provide sufficient privacy when they're pulled down.

The white wicker, woodwork, and small area rug are as important to the success of this room as are the understated hues chosen for the walls and upholstery. The white accents are straightforward, simple, and casually elegant; better still, in this context, they seem to add their own sparkle to the light that fills the room from morning to night.

USING WARM COLORS TO LIGHTEN AND BRIGHTEN

Even a small, windowless corner looks a lot brighter if you color it sunshine yellow; the most ponderous cabinets take on new life if you coat them with a cheerful pastel. If color can do that, imagine what it can do in surroundings that offer more workable built-in beauty.

Even before a color scheme was chosen, the kitchen featured here had lots going for it. The main work area, pictured *at right,* is sleekly contemporary, with state-of-the art appliances and ample yet unobtrusive storage. Directly opposite the work area, the breakfast area, shown *above,* provides comfortable seating in the pleasant shelter of the room's second wraparound window.

Both areas are well planned, but what gives them their special charm is the color scheme. White would have been perfectly acceptable but perhaps a bit cool and bland; yellow would have added warmth in a somewhat predictable way. Instead, the homeowners chose a more adventurous approach. The warm pink they selected for banquettes, chairs, most of the cabinets, and assorted accents adds cheer and charm to what might have been an overly efficient-looking work space.

There's always enough light in this room, thanks to the generous window allotment, an industrial-style hanging fixture above the breakfast table, a series of recessed soffit fixtures, and strip lighting (not shown) on the ceiling. It's the pink-and-cream color scheme, however, that imparts a warm glow, even on rainy days.

LIVING WITH COLOR AND LIGHT

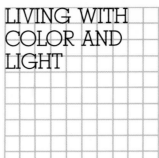

USING COLOR TO CALM AND QUIET

Blue is a restful color. It brings to mind summer skies and tree-ringed lakes. It's anything but a dull color, though, as the serene, elegant living room pictured *at left* shows.

Here, a soft blue of medium intensity provides an interesting yet soothing background for the room's eclectic decorating scheme. The furniture mix is lively, with unexpected accents highlighting its largely traditional look. The blue and white plaid wing chair is a classic component of countless living rooms; the sky blue armchair is centuries younger in style; and finally, the floral-patterned sofa has a bold design that brings drama to its simple lines. The blue walls tie all these elements together.

Although blue is a popular choice, it's by no means the only color to turn to when you're looking for a color scheme that will pull together disparate styles or pieces into one well-fitted unit. Other cool-appearing colors—notably greens, some grays, most (though not all) neutral earth tones, and many pastels—have a similar effect.

White is perhaps the greatest cooler of them all. Whether it's the serenity of a snow-covered hillside in the moonlight or the refreshing contrast of a white trellis against a sunny summer landscape, white is a color that almost inevitably suggests peaceful, calming images.

The room pictured *at left* uses white generously. Here, an elaborately textured white rug balances the crisp white architectural detailing of the walls and the grayed-white painting above the mantel; a white cotton-covered sofa or softly tailored white draperies could produce a similar effect.

Where, when, and how to use quiet colors

Using color to slow down a fast-paced decorating scheme doesn't mean doing without brights and darks, contrasts, and intriguing patterns. Rather, it means knowing what to do when you think the room has about all the colors it can handle. A touch of the right cool, neutral, or pale color can do wonders when calming a vibrant hue or tying two complementary colors together.

If you've boldly painted or papered your walls, for example, in a deep jewel tone, consider using cooler, lighter tones for upholstery. If you're interested in making a small space look roomier and less cluttered, using quiet colors for the large items in the room can do wonders.

In a larger room that has a lot of furniture pieces in a mix of styles, using tints and shades of the same color can help turn a large, busy space into a much more gracious and relaxing one. Keep in mind, too, that you can use white or another background color to disguise unsightly features such as oversize radiators or awkwardly placed jogs in a wall. If you paint such features to blend with the wall color, they'll be less visible.

USING COLOR TO CREATE MOVEMENT

Lots of open spaces, two-story-high ceilings, and clean, simple lines are the key features of the contemporary living area featured here. The angular, vertically oriented architecture is part of the story, of course, but the use of color to help define these striking spaces is at least as important.

The honey-toned parquet floor does more than provide a decorative note—it clearly delineates traffic patterns. Most striking of all are the bright red railings that serve as the focal point around the second-story balcony. As you can tell from the photographs *below* and *at right,* the railings also are important safety features. Painting them red makes them no less functional, but much more fun: They grab attention and direct it upward, emphasizing

the home's dramatic and sophisticated multilevel layout.

The red accents aren't forgotten at ground level. Here, a comfortably upholstered but uncluttered sofa brings vibrant color to the seating area. The richly textured rug, with its assortment of stained-glass reds and oranges, ensures that the floor get its fair share of attention.

Because the design of the home is meant to be appreciated from top to bottom in total, it was especially important to inject color and visual interest in the furnishings to complement, not compete with, the architecture. Even the thriving plants and stark black chimney pipe add to the effect.

MERGING
A ROOM
WITH THE
OUTDOORS

Merging indoor space with the great outdoors is more than a matter of windows: You have to find the right mood out there and bring it inside along with the view. If you aren't taking advantage of a worthy view, consider what a well-placed window or two might add. If you already have a good view, ask yourself if the room's decor helps capture the spirit of the world beyond your walls.

The seaside cottage pictured on these two pages was designed to take full advantage of its surroundings. As the exterior view *above* shows, the home is geared for outdoor living, with a two-level, picket-fenced patio. Two porchlike entries lead from the deck to the cottage's main living level, encouraging an easy transition from indoor to outdoor space.

A room with a view

The semicircular dormer arching from the roof gives the master bedroom, pictured *at right,* a wall-wide seascape. Framed by the curving dormer ceiling and window, the view changes with the tides and times of day, and on clear nights, the telescope commands a panoramic sweep of the heavens and the sea.

Abundant oceanfront light, sparkling white walls uninterrupted even by corners, and soft accent colors create a sense of tranquillity. Look out the window and the mood changes, thanks to ocean waves and changeable colors. Vertical-louvered blinds, stacked to the sides of the big window, can be closed for coziness or to shield against glare.

Spare, clean decorating suits the ambience of this beachfront perch. Every piece of furniture is here to be used; not one blocks the view or changes the mood. Some color accents—notably the soft blue vase and subtle pastel area rug—fit in perfectly with the color of a sunny-day ocean; others, such as the pale hues in the area rug and bedspread, accent the room's airy spaciousness.

BRINGING LIGHT
TO DARK SPACES

Just about every room of your home is likely to be dark at least part of the time; *how* dark and *how much* of the time are the real questions. If you have spaces that get little if any sunlight at any time of day, you probably want to do everything you can to make them seem lighter than they are. If you spend lots of nighttime in one particular room, artificial lighting and light-maximizing decorating become especially important.

Bringing light to a dark room can be as simple as flipping a switch or as multifaceted as the white-on-white color scheme and carefully focused track light system that brighten the living room featured *at left*. The room has windows along one wall (not shown here), so the almost-all-white surroundings make the most of both natural and artificial light. Nubby upholstery, palest-possible beige accessories, bleached hardwood floors, and white storage units are all in keeping with this scheme.

The cozy entertainment center pictured *below* takes a different approach to light. Here, a neutral color scheme also sets the mood. Light beige carpeting covers floors and storage platforms for a smooth, coordinated look. The shiny chrome surfaces of the television, stereo, and video-cassette recorder add sparkle, as do the reflective metal frames of the artwork.

This room is meant primarily for after-dark use, and the owners wanted lots of flexible lighting so they could fine-tune its mood with a series of dimmer switches. Wall-washers recessed into the ceiling highlight the artwork. Eyeball spots, also recessed into the ceiling, dramatize an arrangement of branches in a delicate glass vase and other interesting objets d'art.

UNIFYING ROOMS
WITH COLOR

The living room pictured *at right* is frankly luxurious. It's also eclectic—even daring—in its mix of Oriental and Venetian antiques and contemporary Italian furnishings. The ornate antique chest and chairs, the richly embroidered throw draped over the sofa back, the fragile vases, and the sleekly upholstered sofa and chairs don't, at first glance, appear to have much in common.

What helps bring all these elements together? Color—and careful restraint in using it.

The soft-gray carpeting and equally gentle-hued walls provide an ideal background for the diverse objects so skillfully arrayed here. By using the same unassuming color on the walls and floor over a large area, the homeowner was able to create precisely the unity called for in her varied decorating scheme.

Where she did introduce colorful accents, the blue, pink, and plum tones are grayed just enough to work harmoniously with the main background shade. Even the smaller accessories, such as the silver candlesticks and chrome planter, share the warm gray neutrality of the background.

Your home needn't be filled with a dazzling array of collector's items for this type of color scheming to be useful and workable. If you have an eclectic collection of furniture, using the same color or color family for the upholstery on several pieces or for other accents such as pillows will help tie everything together. If you have a large or L-shape living/dining area, for example, you might choose to furnish them in different styles, but use the same wall or rug color to unify the overall area.

LIVING WITH COLOR AND LIGHT

LIGHTING A KITCHEN FOR MOOD AND EFFICIENCY

No matter how striking a kitchen is, it doesn't do you much good if the lighting doesn't make working there pleasant and safe. Furthermore, no matter how brightly illuminated your food preparation area is, an important element will be missing if the surroundings don't also offer some aesthetic bonuses.

The kitchen/living room combination featured here offers both superefficient lighting and charm. The result is a work and eating area that seems to be gifted with enduring sunlight.

A generous assortment of windows and glass doors provides ample daylighting on all but the dimmest days. The contemporized fanlight above the French doors is an especially appealing touch that scoops in welcome extra light.

Large-scale general lighting is dramatic enough to be a definite decorating plus, yet simple enough not to overwhelm the space. Large hanging fixtures focus on the main work counter and the dining table, shedding more-than-ample light where it's needed; paper shades filter the light without blocking it. A wall-mounted half-cylinder, visible on the exterior oven wall in the photograph *opposite,* adds supplementary task lighting as well as an interesting visual accent.

The well-planned color treatment starts at the bottom, with light-colored wood floors. Soft-yellow walls and the white ceiling and woodwork bounce light, both natural and artificial, back into the kitchen's main activity areas.

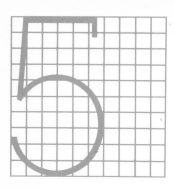

5

ROOMS THAT WORK

Every room needs light, not just for practical purposes but also so that it can be seen to best advantage. Even the most lighthearted pastels, for example, will look bland or even dull if the light is wrong. And a richer, deeper scheme can soon turn murky in unsympathetic light. Both daylight and artificial light affect how colors appear. More than that, they affect your sense of the entire room—its shape, size, angles, and mood. In this chapter, you'll see how light and color work together to turn 13 rooms into superb spaces.

HOW LIGHT AFFECTS YOUR SENSE OF SPACE

A sunny room with lots of windows almost always looks larger and better-proportioned than it really is; the same can be true for a softly lit room with few windows, if the lamps or fixtures are well-chosen. It's not so much a question of what kind of light as of how the light is used and focused.

Light coming from unexpected places such as heights and angles can lend an exciting quality to even a conventionally arranged space. When the space itself also is something out of the ordinary, light can do even more.

The vaulted entryway pictured *at right,* flanked by a window-walled home office and a dining room, combines abundant natural light with imaginative architecture. The soaring ceiling would give a sense of generous space under most circumstances; here, it gets additional help from its surroundings. The ceiling's height and impact are emphasized by a long window that extends upward from what would be the conventional ceiling line and reaches nearly to the ceiling's peak.

The wood-accented window walls that shape the entry repeat the style of the exterior windows and are important to the home's unified look. Much of the ground floor benefits from the light, airy quality created by the glass front. The interior window walls provide some sense of separation between the living area, eating area, and office, without blocking out light or appealing outdoor vistas. The result is spacious and open, with a welcome touch of warmth and enclosure.

THE DYNAMICS OF COLOR AND LIGHT

Bright colors and bright light seem to go together; so, too, do soft colors and soft light. That's not to say that gentle pastels and rich jewel tones have no place in a light-drenched room, or that clear primaries will be out of place in a room with few windows. These and other variations can work if you remember that light and color depend on each other. Consider light source and light quality as you choose your colors. As long as you keep this light and color interrelationship in mind, you won't have to worry about dark tones looking dull in a dim setting or paler tints seeming washed out in strong sun.

The spaces pictured here are almost enough to make solid geometry seem glamorous. The combination of unexpected soaring angles, dramatic shafts of sunlight, and high, light-colored ceilings creates a setting that turns lessons about pyramids and cubes into decorating magic. It's not just the geometry, though, that makes these areas special. Here, color and light work together to bring even more drama to an already dramatic scheme.

In the open-plan living room/ dining room/kitchen pictured *opposite,* the interplay between architecture, light, and furnishings is especially effective. The multiangled ceiling shapes a light and shadow pattern; subtle tints overhead and on some of the walls—pale peach and delicate cornflower blue—further emphasize the ceiling's impact. The colors, partially repeated in the upholstery fabrics, almost suggest that the sun is creating the color scheme, as it might outdoors in a scenic sunset.

There's even more dazzling light—and architecture—here than meets the eye. The sofa in the living area faces a floor-to-ceiling window that, when it reaches the top of the room, angles over to form an inverted L and leads to a row of clerestory windows. These in turn bring in even more light through the post-supported projecting wall that hovers protectively over the piano.

Color-coded zoning
Using different colors, however subtly, also helps define the function of each section of the main living area pictured here. Note how the white walls in the living and dining areas, as well as the projecting triangular windows at the junction of those two "rooms," help mark the transition between the unpartitioned zones.

The hallway shown *at left* uses the same color motifs as the larger parts of the living area. The ceiling lines, too, are part of the overall plan that you see on a larger scale in the other photograph. Here, the narrowness of the space is both emphasized and made less potentially oppressive by means of soft color and abundant light.

Practical purposes
The small, somewhat unexpected window facing the seafoam-painted stair railing helps lighten the sense of enclosure the hallway might otherwise convey. What's more, the window provides necessary light during the day at the base of the stairs, an area where good visibility always is important. (At night, overhead lights, not in view here, provide the margin of safety.)

ADDING LIGHT
IN UNEXPECTED WAYS

There are lots of ways to bring additional light into a room. Windows, skylights, translucent window treatments, and extra lamps and fixtures are all familiar standbys. The effort (and expense) you go to have something to do with the effect you get. The key variable, however, is how you approach the light sources: unusual placement or imaginative combinations of components can add decorative flair as well as needed illumination to your home.

The cathedral-ceilinged living room shown *opposite* reaches for the sky in every way. Not only are most of its decorative accessories strongly vertical, but the entire roof really is a skylight, which allows daylight to flood the room from sunrise to sunset. The result of this unexpected switch in materials, from solid to see-through, is a wide-open look in keeping with the room's sophisticated/frontier styling.

The room pictured *below* is less unusual at first glance. On a floor plan, it would look fairly standard: windows flanking a fireplace on an end wall and French doors highlighting the exterior sidewall. When you see the room itself, however, the effect is quite different.

The fireside windows, rather than the traditional small squares nestled above a pair of bookcases or a half-wall of paneling, are unusually tall and handsome. In addition to the conventionally sized casements in each window's midsection, there are top and bottom transomlike elements. As a result, natural light floods the room throughout the day.

Because this home is in the Southwest, where the sun is especially strong, the homeowners had to find a way to limit light as well as allow for it. Here, light-controlling miniblinds, pulled all the way up in the photograph, perform that role efficiently.

As these examples show, both minor changes in size, scale, and placement of light sources and dramatic changes in major architectural elements can add light in unexpected ways. If you think your house needs brightening, let imagination be your guide.

USING COLOR AND LIGHT TO TIE SPACES TOGETHER

Threads of color and streams of light are more than turns of phrase—taken literally, they can help you smooth the architectural ups and downs and harsh corners and edges at your house. Consider, for example, easing the threat of a cluttered look in a small space with a simple, restful color scheme. Or emphasize the relationship of two rooms—or even levels—by letting them share a dramatic light source, such as a hallway skylight. Whether you have a small space that seems even smaller because it's fractured into several use and color zones or several larger areas that you'd like to relate to each other better, color and its constant companion, light, can be great unifiers.

The sunset-hued dining area pictured *at left* is a clearly defined space in its own right. It's also related closely enough to the expansive living area in the background to make the whole effect seem even more appealing than each of its parts. The key, of course, is color.

Here, restful gray-violet walls and floors set both a color scheme and a mood throughout the main living level. The painting on the wall introduces bolder versions of the same color and helps define the transition to the living room, where slightly brighter and darker pinks and purples take over from the subdued tones that dominate the dining area.

The sculptural metal stairway, imaginatively placed where a dividing wall might have been in a more traditionally styled home, provides an important color note, too. Painted a slightly lighter version of the lacquered burgundy that coats the pillar in the living room, it leads the eye upward again, this time to the second floor. The stairway thus serves as both an unusual room divider and an important component of the overall color scheme.

Lighting also plays a part in tying the large open areas together, though its initial impact is more subtle. Abundant natural light filtering through vertical blinds illuminates both the living and dining areas. At night or on dark days, a carefully planned light system takes over. Recessed lighting in the dining area provides soft illumination at mealtimes; cove lighting around the perimeter of the living area continues the subtle light-from-above theme. Bright highlights come from a few strategically arranged canister fixtures.

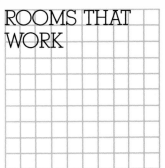

BRINGING LIGHT AND COLOR TO INTERIOR SPACES

Not all rooms have windows or even exterior walls in which window openings can be made. The advantage of such a room is a greater-than-usual amount of wall space—an aid when it comes to arranging furniture or appliances and finding hanging room for decorative items. As far as getting a fair share of light, however, interior spaces have to try much harder. The results of a successful effort can be dazzling.

There are several ways to open up an inside room to the expansive feeling that abundant daylight brings. The center-of-the-house kitchen pictured *at left* exemplifies two of them.

First of all, although it is an interior space, it's not completely blocked off from the rest of the house. The wall housing cabinets and open-shelf storage visually separates the kitchen from the living room, but doesn't reach the ceiling. The divider that defines the dining area, which is just out of camera range to the right, is low enough to permit conversation between people in the kitchen and those at the table, but high enough to conceal kitchen clutter. Both partitions are positioned so that light that floods the exterior spaces, thanks to the living room's window wall, also can peek into the kitchen.

Color has a major role here, too. Using solid yellow for the counters and cabinets and clean white for just about everything else in the kitchen suggests sunshine even on the cloudiest day.

Because this home is mostly on one level, the owners were able to install a large skylight where it would do the most good: It's strategically located above the living room/kitchen divider and provides abundant light to both rooms. In a two-story house, or one where a skylight isn't feasible for other reasons, a good alternative might be to install a row of clerestory windows high on the exterior wall of a first-floor room. Light from those could shine over an interior half-wall into a dining room, kitchen, or family room.

LETTING THE SETTING PROVIDE COLOR AND LIGHT

No matter where you live, whether it's a tree-lined suburban street, a wooded hillside, or a level lot with a good view of the sky, you may be able to bring color and light from the outside into your home. A view of changing clouds through a clerestory window or seasonal foliage through a French door could be every bit as decorative as the most carefully chosen wall hangings. If you're building a new home, encourage the designer to take the setting into account when considering both the floor plan and window placement. If you live in an older home, take a good look at all the existing windows and see if there's a view you'd like to see more of.

If your home is surrounded by tall trees and few neighboring homes, it makes excellent sense to take advantage of those assets. The two-story-high living room pictured *at right* does just that. Dazzling expanses of glass on three sides of the room bring inside the beauty of the natural setting as well as abundant natural light.

In spring, summer, and fall, the trees themselves add a vibrant and varied touch of color to the simple white-and-earth-tone scheme. In winter, when the trees lose their leaves, the view of branches against the sky adds to the impact of the room's elegantly understated decor. At all seasons, thriving plants, placed at several points in the room and benefiting from the room's abundant sunlight, heighten the sense that the outdoors has been brought indoors.

The white surfaces of the walls and ceilings make the most of the light that floods the room. Because privacy is not a concern here, window treatments are unnecessary; the walls, too, are left largely unadorned.

Note that the "windows" are really sliding glass doors—less expensive alternatives to the custom windows that would have been needed to fit these large openings. Just like conventionally placed patio doors, these can be opened in warm weather to let in cooling breezes. The owners operate them with a window pole.

PLAYING LIGHT OFF SURFACES

The brightest sunlight or lamplight will be dimmed if the surfaces it shines on are dark and color-absorbent, with low- or no-gloss finishes. To get the most out of a room's illumination, whatever its source, consider surfaces—walls, floors, ceilings, even furnishings themselves—that will reflect and highlight available light. Both color and texture play a part in the selection process, as the room pictured here demonstrates.

The family room/den pictured *at right* is elegant, spacious, and comfortable. What it does lack, however, is well-distributed window space. One window, out of camera range, is on the wall to the right of the leather chairs; additional daylight reaches the room through sliding glass doors in the distance to the rear left.

Much of the room needs to be lit artificially at certain times of day as well as at night. Several features help this room get the most benefit from an elaborate track light system and the unevenly distributed daylight.

Perhaps the most noticeable aspect of the room is how shiny—yet nonglaring—it is. Custom-built cabinets of satin-finish stainless steel and highly polished oak provide an ideal surface for reflective light. They sparkle in direct light, glow in indirect light, and add interest to the setting.

Other features performing a similar role include pipe-style supports for the track lights and a glazed tile floor; the tile brings warm color to the surroundings, too.

The designer also selected furnishings that would reflect light. Cylindrical end tables and chrome-base chairs have shiny surfaces. The leather of the chairs, too, is smooth and somewhat glossy, and its light-to-medium colors add to the room's light-maximizing properties. Only the soft gray rug fails to reflect light; instead it adds a restful quality to a room that's dazzling with direct, indirect, and reflected light.

PLANNING A HOUSE AROUND COLOR AND LIGHT

Planning your own home offers a wonderful opportunity to initiate your own design ideas. It gives you the chance to emphasize what's important to you, whether that's an open floor plan that suits an informal life-style, or a particular room arrangement and color scheme that complement both the architecture and the setting. Although building a brand-new house is one way to start fresh, it's not the only way. Here and on the next two pages, we'll show you a house that was remodeled from top to bottom, always with a thoughtful eye toward the effects and interplay of color and light.

The home featured here was built over a decade ago. Tucked onto a steeply sloping lot, it was originally a two-bedroom structure featuring standard-size, standard-height rooms. When an interior designer and his wife purchased this house, they decided to transform it into a combined home and office.

To achieve the kind of interior zoning they needed for private living and working space, they removed some walls and built others, creating half-levels within the house. This put the entry on-grade, one office a few steps up from there, and the main living core a full level up from the entry; on the fourth level there is a master suite and secondary office space.

Aside from a radical change in the traffic patterns, perhaps the most striking result of this remodeling is the way light is coaxed into virtually all parts of the house. Because of its hillside site, the house gets sun for only about half of the day; at other times sunlight is blocked by the top of the hill. Thanks to the new floor plan, skylights and high-on-the-wall windows bring in every bit of available daylight.

The high-ceilinged, big-windowed living room pictured *opposite* is perhaps the most dramatic room in the house. White walls and deep-blue upholstery make a striking combination all by themselves. With the added impact of wide-open spaces and unexpected niches, the effect is even more impressive.

The two-story plate-glass window that provides a view of the garden was part of the remodeling project. Originally, there was only a small, horizontal crank-operated window here. Replacing that with an extra-large one opened up the whole wall, and the whole room. For even greater impact, this window was bumped out 12 inches. Mirrors on the sides and top of the bump-out give intriguing double reflections from every angle.

The other half of the living room, which doubles as a dining area, is pictured *at left*. Here you can see another innovative use of windows— a series of clerestories that cast additional light on the fireplace corner. Note the turquoise rock on the mantel and the more subtly hued bowl on the marble coffee table. These seemingly minor accessories were carefully chosen to pick up the turquoise accents used architecturally throughout the house. *(continued)*

PLANNING A HOUSE AROUND COLOR AND LIGHT

(continued)

There's more to lighting a house than sunshine, of course. To brighten the loft/music room pictured *opposite,* as well as the living room shown on the two preceding pages, the homeowner/designer used track lighting—lots of it.

Because each light canister can be turned in any direction, this type of lighting is ideal not just for general room illumination but also for highlighting specific items. Look to the left of the L-shaped seating unit and you can see another way the designer provided accent lighting. The side table, a translucent plastic cylinder, also is a light that plays up the hand-blown amber glass vase

on top of it. Even at night, with other lights off, this illuminated piece of furniture warms the loft with a mellow glow.

As you look at this restful room you can see how the color scheme initiated on the level below has been carried out here, too. The white walls serve as a backdrop for white, rather than blue, natural-fiber upholstery. This time, the deep blue, as well as a trace of soft turquoise, appear in company with other small doses of rich colors in the wall hanging and throw pillows.

A recurring theme

The view toward the kitchen, pictured *at lower left,* shows a striking reappearance of the vi-

brant blue used so effectively in the living room and so subtly in the loft. This time, the surface is laminated rather than painted, making the kitchen as practical as it is dramatic. White marble countertops provide abundant work space and contrast crisply with the unexpected deep tones of the cabinets. Here, too, track lights are used to provide flexible task and general lighting.

The master bedroom shown *at lower right* reverses the color scheme of the living room. Here, the intense blue is used on the walls (thanks to a generously sprayed application of high-gloss auto lacquer); the white is used for furniture, notably the platform bed. There's

also a trace of the hallmark turquoise—this time it's visible in the upper left portion of the photograph, along the track of the sliding window panel covering glass doors that divide the master bedroom from the loft.

To make the most of this room's sculptural spaces and unusual colors, the homeowner/designer installed recessed lighting beneath the bed's platform. The same 7-watt Christmas tree bulbs used beneath the bed also are used on top of the soffit for additional ambient lighting.

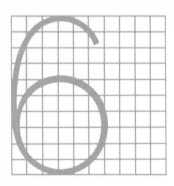

6

PLANNING LIGHTING

As you've seen in the preceding chapters, both lighting and color are decorating tools. To an even greater extent than color, however, lighting is more than just a pretty face: In its natural and artificial forms, light is a vital, practical component of any home. Often, the most effective lighting combines good looks with efficiency. When you're planning lighting, it's a good idea to start with function, then go on to appearance once you've narrowed down your needs. In this chapter, we'll show you how to plan general lighting for whole rooms and narrow hallways, task lighting for eye-straining work, accent lighting for wall hangings or pieces of art, mood lighting for gardens, and much more.

GENERAL ILLUMINATION

General illumination is just what it sounds like—lighting that covers all or a good part of a room and doesn't play favorites. It's there for safety and practical reasons, so you can see where you're going, who you're talking to, what your surroundings look like. Good general illumination means even lighting—no glare, no arbitrary bright spots, no shadows to interrupt the view.

During the day, sunlight coming through windows, skylights, or even glass-paned doors can be an excellent source of general illumination. Glare may be a problem if the sunlight strikes a polished floor or piece of furniture, or, worse still, a mirror. If glare is a factor at some times of the day, or certain seasons when the sun is low in the sky, consider using almost-sheer curtains or adjustable interior shutters to filter the light.

Even during the day, not all rooms get sufficient sun to eliminate the need for artificial light; at night, all rooms need help. To provide general illumination when nature does not, built-in and attached fixtures are among the best options, though not the only ones, as you'll see later in the chapter.

The smoothly lit, sleekly furnished living room pictured *at right* benefits from several light sources. On bright days, ample light comes in through the unadorned windows above the window seat and through the dramatic window placed high on the wall in the upper left portion of the photograph. When daylight isn't sufficient or available, the track system that hugs the room's perimeter provides abundant, well-distributed light. *(continued)*

GENERAL
ILLUMINATION
(continued)

General illumination isn't necessarily bright, functional, or harsh. For many purposes, such as entertaining, soft, almost dusk-like lighting is pleasanter and more popular. In a heavily used room, flexible general illumination is both a decorative and a practical plus.

The rooms pictured here show two very different styles of fixtures, united by one important feature: The light from both the ornate dining room chandelier and the understated built-ins in the living room can be made as bright or as soft as the homeowners wish. The key to this versatility is a widely available device known as a dimmer switch, or rheostat.

The fixtures shown here are operated by wall switches in which dimmers have been installed. Replacing a standard switch with a dimmer is usually a routine do-it-yourself operation. Be sure, however, that the dimmer you're installing can handle at least the total wattage of the fixture or fixtures it will govern; most dimmers have a 600-watt capacity.

The most familiar dimmer switches have a round center knob—you push it in to turn the light on or off and turn it clockwise or counterclockwise to adjust the brightness; dimmers that look like conventional toggle switches are increasingly common, however. If you explore your local lighting center you'll find other types of dimmers, too, both for wall-mounting and for attaching to lamp sockets or cords.

Incidentally, although dimmers are almost always installed with the primary goal of adjusting light levels, they bring other benefits with them. The first is energy efficiency: Bulbs that are burned at less than their maximum brightness use less electricity. What's more, they last much longer, providing a second economy.

(continued)

GENERAL ILLUMINATION
(continued)

There are times when general illumination doubles as task lighting and the main concern is efficiency, rather than shading and flexibility. Kitchens are perhaps the brightest examples of settings where super-practical general lighting is a necessity.

The sleekly contemporary kitchen pictured *opposite* shows how attractive this emphasis on efficiency can be. Here, large industrial-style ceiling fixtures provide ample overall lighting for basic kitchen chores such as cooking and cleanup. A string of small

wall-mounted bulbs supplements the overhead lights for tasks such as chopping, slicing, or reading recipes that require more illumination.

In addition to abundant lighting, this kitchen has several light-enhancing features that make the most of the light provided by the fixtures. Notice, for instance, the glossy, pale gray laminate cabinets, shiny white ceramic-tile counters, and light-reflective white ceiling, all of which more than balance the darker, richer, light-absorbing tones of the quarry-tile floor.

1 The quality of light provided by a pendant lamp such as the one pictured here depends upon the type of shade or globe used and the fixture's height above the floor. Light intensity tends to drop off beyond a small circle—although not as abruptly as the diagram suggests—with this kind of fixture.

2 The ceiling-mounted fixture pictured here provides enough light for safe passage through the space; it's not a source of high-level light. Even used in groups, ceiling mounts are less efficient than down-

lights and are best for low-level general lighting.

3 These recessed downlights are grouped so that light patterns overlap to provide good, even illumination. Downlights allow you to match fixture type with bulb type, such as reflectors or floods, to achieve the lighting levels needed.

4 Track lights, like those pictured here, let you adjust the direction and number of light patterns, as well as the sizes of bulbs, to provide the optimum general light level.

TASK LIGHTING

When you're doing something that requires you to see every detail without straining, you need brighter, better-focused light than even the best general illumination can provide. That's when task lighting becomes important.

Wall-mounted fixtures, well-aimed track lights, versatile built-ins, and familiar table and floor lamps all provide effective task lighting. Which type you choose depends primarily on the look you want; size and placement determine how large and how intensely an area is lit.

The chrome swing-arm wall fixture that illuminates the kitchen planning center pictured *opposite* only lights a limited part of the room, so there's no need for it to be any larger than it is. (Other parts of the kitchen are abundantly lit by other sources, as you can see on pages 60 and 61.)

The wall fixture here is placed so that it provides a pool of bright light at the center of the work area, just right for hand-writing notes or reading cookbooks. When the computer is in use, the swing-arm allows the fixture to be moved to one side to maintain the necessary light level but avoid glare on the screen.

The industrial-style pendant fixture in the breakfast corner pictured *at right* has a more limited function: It's just a light to dine by, and on sunny days enough light comes through the window to make even this light unnecessary. This fixture, therefore, doesn't need to be as flexible as the wall fixture in the planning center.

For more about planning task lighting, see page 100 and pages 108–121 (Chapter 7— "A Lighting Primer.")

(continued)

A s the breakfast corner pictured on the preceding page suggests, task lighting isn't just for homework and housework: It's for anything that requires good visibility. The well-planned bathroom featured *below* is further evidence of that.

In this lavishly tiled bath, there are several use zones, and each—has its own light source—or sources. Above the tub, out of camera range, there's a round, recessed built-in fixture. The pair of sinks, separated by a fold-down storage bin and shelf for toiletries,

each boast not one but two task lights. For shaving and other grooming activities, there are recessed fluorescent panels above each mirror. For added brightness, there's a small fluorescent tube tucked under the shelf above each of the sinks.

The lighting for the dining table and banquette pictured *opposite* offers fewer surprises, but is equally contemporary in approach. Here, a track system equipped with several types of fixtures lights the table and highlights wall hangings and accessories.

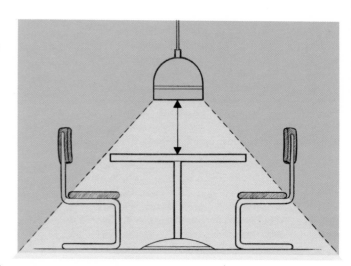

The distance between the work surface and the bottom of the light source is the key to achieving proper task-light levels; about 25 inches usually is considered optimum. The size of the area to be lit is less easy to pinpoint, however.

If you want to cover a whole table with light, you might choose a fixture with a broadly flared shade; for a smaller area, a more compact fixture or more confining shade might be more efficient.

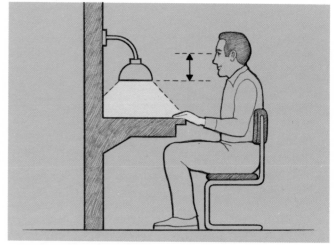

Avoiding glare is especially important when you're planning task lighting; check the user's eye level before installing a fixture or lamp. Then place the light source so that no glare reaches the user's eyes; the ideal level for the light source

usually is about 10 to 12 inches below eye level. When you select a fixture, be sure the diffuser, or shade, will eliminate any shadows cast by other light sources. An adjustable lamp or fixture is especially helpful for this purpose.

ACCENT
LIGHTING

Accent lighting is the most purely decorative of the main types of illumination. It might almost be described as makeup for your home: Its role is to highlight displays of attractive accessories, to illuminate carefully arranged furniture groupings in cozy corners, to dramatize architectural detailing, and to accent whatever else it takes to show off your home's best features.

It doesn't necessarily take a lot of light to accomplish this decorative task, but just how much depends on what you want to accent. The display of glassware in the dining room pictured *at left,* for example, seems at first to owe its prominence primarily to three small, recessed downlights. Look more closely, though, and you'll see that the shelves' mirrored backing multiplies the impact of those lights, and adds reflections of ceiling-mounted spotlights along the adjacent wall. What's more, there's a row of small bulbs tucked under the storage unit's base to provide a dramatic wash of light in the space below the shelves.

The accent lighting in the living room pictured *opposite* is quite different in scale, as well as effect. Here, the star is the large folding screen between the sofa and the shuttered window. During the day, sunlight provides all the accent light that's necessary. It filters through the shutters, highlighting every detail of the screen's striking geometric design.

At night, two floor-level uplights perform the same role. They provide almost no light in the room itself—that function is well served by the floor lamps that flank the sofa—but once again they do turn the screen into a dramatic backdrop for the entire room.   *(continued)*

ACCENT LIGHTING
(continued)

Accent lighting and artwork are almost inseparable, because artwork needs to be showcased, sometimes subtly, sometimes assertively. The long, narrow hallway pictured *opposite* exemplifies the subtle approach.

The floor is a key component of a three-sided arrangement of treasured ethnic rugs that has turned an awkward and rather claustrophobic space into a gallery of textile art. A row of bowl-shape, wall-mounted uplights creates a soft general light that illuminates the hallway and gently accents the textures of the

rugs. During the day they're accented in a different way—by natural light that filters through mini-slat blinds shading the windows on the exterior wall.

The miniature entertainment center pictured *below* illustrates another application of accent lighting. Again, daylight, when available, is important; the light coming through a window on the opposite wall—reflected in the cabinet below the TV set—provides necessary illumination. Soft cove lighting that wraps around the entire room provides a decorative yet practical glow that's ideal for evening television viewing.

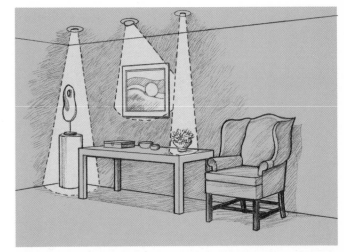

Ceiling-mounted accent lighting, either recessed or surface, can be adjusted to point in precisely the direction you wish. The light spread—that is, the shape and intensity—varies according to fixture type, as the drawing above indicates. Eyeballs, pinspots, and half-louvers are among the most widely used; wall washers, which also are commonly available, provide general as well as accent lighting.

The drawing above shows a form of accent illumination known as valance indirect lighting. Designed to bounce off walls and ceilings, it's ideal for accenting architectural features, wall-hung textiles, and other artwork. This type of accent lighting often is built in, but you can purchase fixtures that will provide much the same effect in smaller or more confined areas.

LIGHTING OUTDOOR LIVING AREAS

One of the great pleasures of having even the tiniest yard is being able to spend time outdoors whenever you're at home. Whether your favorite outdoor pastimes consist of active work and recreation, or pure relaxation, you probably begrudge every moment spent indoors in good weather. Fortunately, with well-planned exterior lighting, you won't need to limit your outdoor living to daylight hours.

The multilevel deck pictured *at left* shows one way to create an outdoor living room. Floodlights mounted on the side of the house provide bright overall lighting. They're well above eye level, avoiding annoying glare; in addition, they're deliberately angled to shine directly on the potted geraniums and pansies that border the deck, so that even at night the warm colors can be seen clearly.

To further enhance the deck's versatility, its uppermost level is set up as a snack-and-conversation area, and the middle level is left unfurnished so that children can play on it freely. A moonlike dome light, mounted in a decorative vertical section of the deck, provides area lighting in the "living room."

Although this deck's organization lends itself well to use as full-fledged outdoor living space, the lighting that makes it so pleasant a retreat on warm evenings could be used in other outdoor settings, including a backyard lawn or a masonry patio. You might want to choose portable fixtures of varying heights to illuminate different areas; if you're too far from the house for building-mounted floodlights to cast sufficient light, you might want to install them on a ground-based fixture as well.

Practical considerations

Because outdoor electrical connections are exposed to the weather—notably to moisture—they call for extra precautions. Local codes vary and the electrician who's doing the work should be thoroughly aware of both legal and safety requirements. In general, however, outdoor wiring must be protected by heavy-duty, moisture-resistant sheathed cable and ground-fault circuit interrupters (GFCIs). The cable must either be buried or, if it's near the surface, protected by rigid conduit.

An alternative to standard wiring is low-voltage wiring, which is reduced by a transformer from standard 125-volt household current to a safe level (sometimes as little as 6 volts). Because of this, low-voltage lighting presents little danger of shock or fire even if the wires are damaged by moisture or garden implements. Low-voltage fixtures for outdoor use are widely available at home centers and garden shops.

You may feel that nighttime outdoor living is fine if you can live in an enchanted bug-free climate, but this isn't the case at your house. It's certainly true that moths and other flying creatures can severely limit your enjoyment of the outdoors after dark, and they *are* attracted by lights. If flying insects are a problem at your house, consider adding an electric bug killer to your outdoor lighting scheme. These units use black light to attract bugs. Some then use high-voltage electricity or water to destroy them; other devices drown them.

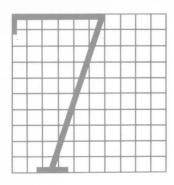

7

A LIGHTING PRIMER

Walk into any lighting store and you'll find a bewildering array of lamps and fixtures on display—sometimes so many that individual styles and sizes get lost in the crowd. Presented with such an abundance of options, where do you start and how do you decide what to buy? To begin, define your lighting needs and style preferences. Try to narrow your choices before you go shopping so that you'll know whether you should focus on table lamps, floor lamps, track systems, or maybe just shades. This chapter will help you get started by introducing you to the varied selection of lamps and fixtures to be found in stores across the country.

WHERE TO START

From department and furniture stores to discounters, mail-order catalogs, and lighting specialty shops like the one pictured *at right,* there are lots of places to look for lighting ideas.

Before you go shopping, though, survey the room or rooms where you're planning to update lighting. Do you want light for reading or handiwork, strictly for mood, or both? Do you need to highlight a prized accessory item, such as a painting or a piece of pottery? Do you want a new dining room fixture because the old one is the "wrong" style for a new table and chairs? Perhaps you need new lighting because there are too many dark corners in a hallway or family room.

Once you've identified the basis of your need for lighting, you're ready to look for specific lighting products. As with other furnishings, style is important. Whether country charm or contemporary sophistication is the hallmark of your home, you'll be able to find many types of lighting accessories to complement your furnishings.

Light versus shade
Don't overlook the importance of shades; they're more than decorative accessories. If general illumination is your goal, look for translucent, light-tone shades. If you want drama and more sharply defined beams, consider opaque shades. Keep shade style in mind, too. A burlap-covered shade, for example, won't suit a formal setting or a graceful brass urn lamp; a silk shade won't be at home in a family room or on a sturdy earthenware jug lamp. Avoid plopping a large shade on a lamp that's too small for it—the result will be top-heavy both visually and physically.

TABLE LAMPS

Perhaps the most familiar portable light sources, table lamps come in a wide range of styles, from classic ginger-jar bases to colonial candlesticks to contemporary flex-arm models. The lamps pictured here represent just the contemporary end of the spectrum, but illustrate a variety of functions.

The white, translucent-shaded lamps not only provide light for reading but also shed a wide enough glow to qualify as general illuminators. The low base of the lamp *at near right,* however, makes it better suited for a dresser or hall table than for an end table.

Adjustable flex-arm lamps like those shown *at far right* are highly versatile. Their movable elbows and adjustable heads allow them to cast either accent or task light.

Small lamps, such as the white dome light, the black "parson's-hat" lamp, and the spherical black lamp are ideal for turning a dark shelf into a bright eye-catcher; the small black lamps also serve for desk work. The canister-style uplight *at near right,* although designed for floor use, also works well on a table.

When you select table lamps, keep proportion and function as well as style in mind. An especially tall or chunky lamp will look wrong—and be precarious—on a small or low table; a low or skinny lamp will be dwarfed atop a large end table. Even more important, a lamp that's too high will shine in your eyes; one that's too low will light the table beneath it rather than the book you're reading or the seating area you're occupying. Ideally, the bottom of a table lamp shade should be at eye level (38 to 42 inches above the floor) when you're seated.

110

Although floor lamps come in a range of styles and include designs with fixed shades as well as types with detachable shades, certain aspects remain constant. Most important, perhaps, is the need for a stable base and a well-proportioned design. Once those criteria have been met, style and specific function become the key concerns.

Floor lamps are most often used for reading and general lighting; to be as versatile as possible, they often come equipped with dimmers or three-way switches. Some, however, like the three shown *at near left*, have adjustable heads instead. When they're not being used for reading, they can be turned sideways to highlight accessories on a nearby tabletop or wall. Some adjustable-head lamps can be turned into uplights, as well.

Torchères, like the white and black lamps shown third and sixth from the left, are full-time uplights and represent a stylish alternative to standard-shade floor lamps. Their beams bounce off the ceiling, providing drama, general illumination, and the illusion of higher ceilings.

Floor lamps come in a wide range of heights. Generally, the base height measures 40 to 49 inches from the bottom of the shade to the floor.

If you plan to use a floor lamp primarily as a reading light, here are some numbers to keep in mind. Relatively short floor lamps—those from 40 to 42 inches high—should be positioned to line up with your shoulder when you're seated. Taller lamps should be set about 15 inches to the side of the hypothetical book's center and about 20 inches behind it.

Whether you prefer intricate chandeliers or straightforward contemporary designs, hanging lamps can help you meet a variety of lighting needs.

Perhaps the most familiar setting for hanging lamps is the dining room. If that's the location you have in mind, be sure you don't position a chandelier or pendant too near the ceiling. Instead, hang it about 30 inches above the table. If the fixture has an open bottom and is fitted with a bare bulb, be sure to hang the fixture low enough so you light the table surface without casting light in diners' eyes.

If your table is used for more than dining, use a hanging light with a rise-and-fall fitting that lets you adjust the position of the light to suit changing needs. The diameter of your hanging light should be at least a foot less than that of the table beneath it.

Other uses
Besides dining rooms, hanging lights can lend a glow to nightstands, desks, end tables, even kitchen islands. Use a single one over a small table, or hang them two or more over an especially long table or counter. For reading in a chair or in bed, position a

hanging light with its lower
edge about four feet from the
floor. (Test it before hanging; if
the light hits you in the eye,
lower it; if its beam spread
misses your book, raise it.) For
desk work, hang the fixture
with its lower edge 15 inches
above the desktop.

Mounting options
Hanging lights usually drop
straight from a ceiling box, but
what if there's no box where
you want the lamp? One alternative to a costly rewiring job
is to run ceiling track to the
point where you want to drop
the light, then hang the lamp

from the track using a special
"pendant" adapter.
    No ceiling box available? In
that case, tap power from a
wall outlet by discreetly running a cord up a corner and
along the ceiling line. The cord
could feed a swag lamp hung
from a hook in the ceiling or a
plug-in-style track.

115

BUILT-IN LIGHTING

When you want unobtrusive lighting, built-in styles—ranging from completely recessed fixtures to canisters that protrude slightly from the ceiling—may be your best bet. Depending on the type of fixture, its placement, and the type of bulb used, built-ins can provide both general and accent lighting.

Built-in lights, like those pictured here, generally have clean lines and a contemporary appearance, but their simplicity and small size help

them fit into updated older homes as well as into new construction.

Types of built-ins

Circular or square *open-bottom downlights,* like those pictured *at far right,* are ideal for highlighting a wall hanging or large painting, or emphasizing an unusual wall texture. Ideally, you should position downlights 8 to 16 inches from the wall and 18 to 30 inches from each other. To get more general light from this type of fixture,

use flood bulbs and install one recessed light for every 25 square feet of floor space.

For an even wash of light on a wall, ideally when you want to show off a large grouping of artwork, choose wall-washers like the two fixtures at the center of the photograph; these minimize the cone-shape halo that other lights shed on a wall.

Pinspots, like the second fixture from the left, are fitted with a cover that has a small hole in it; this small opening

produces a tight beam of light that can be directed at small treasures.

Eyeballs, pictured at far left, have a half-round projection that moves to adjust the direction of the light. Direct the light downward, use flood bulbs, and you can light a hallway or a large game table; direct it at about a 30-degree angle toward the wall, use a spotlight bulb, and you can highlight artwork.

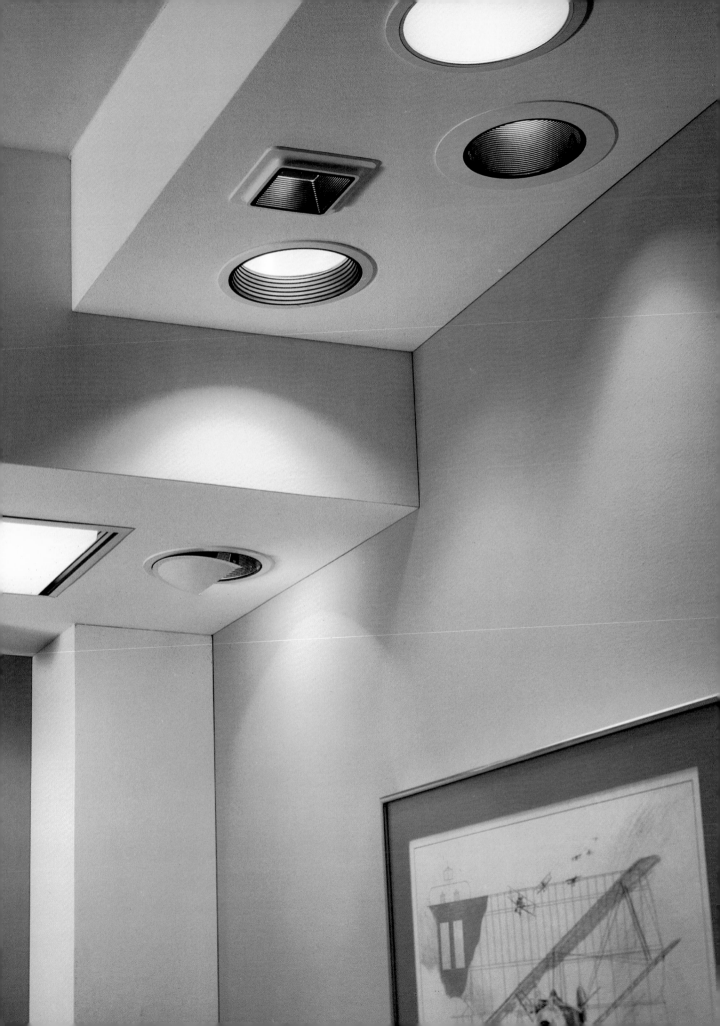

TRACK LIGHTING

Similar in function to built-ins, track lighting adds bold graphic impact to any room and is much easier to install.

Although track systems can be used for general lighting, they're at their best when used for drama. Positioned two to three feet from a standard-height wall, track fixtures can be fitted with narrow-beam spotlights to pick out individual artworks, or wider floods for a general wash of light.

Up-to-the-minute low-voltage track systems offer energy savings and intense, controlled beams of light. Built-in transformers let the fixtures operate on a mere 5.5 to 12 volts of current, instead of the usual 120 volts. Depending on the low-voltage bulb you select, a low-voltage track fixture can produce a narrow light beam to accent a small figurine, or a wider but equally intense beam to dramatize a painting.

As an alternative to track lights placed near the wall, you can center and aim them downward for safe passage through a once-dark hallway, or bounce their light off the walls to turn the hall into a glowing gallery. For contempo-

rary dining drama, center a track above a long rectangular table and aim two or three 50-watt reflector spotlights directly down upon the table.

Consider hanging track lights on a wall, too. For instance, mount a track vertically next to a reading chair: Aim one spotlight at your reading material, bounce one off the ceiling for general lighting, and turn another sideways to highlight a nearby poster.

A piece of track can be the beginning of a great bathroom redo, too. Mount track above or flanking a mirror for a bright new look.

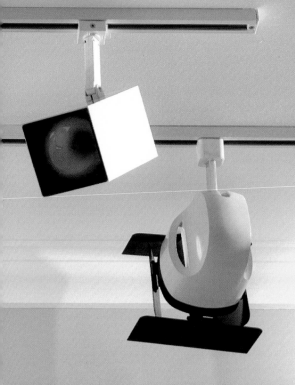

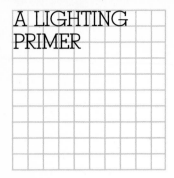

LIGHT BULBS, TUBES, AND ENERGY EFFICIENCY

Time was when a light bulb was a light bulb, and about the only choice you had was which wattage to select. Today, lighting stores, and even the light bulb sections of grocery stores, are brimming with choices. Select the right ones, and you can beautify your home *and* cut your electrical consumption.

Incandescent lighting

Incandescent light is produced today in much the same way it was when Thomas Edison devised the first commercially feasible bulbs nearly a century ago. Electrical current passes through a filament, heating it to the glowing point and resulting in the cozy, yellow-tinted glow we've come to associate with home lighting.

Although incandescent lighting can be dimmed inexpensively, it does consume a relatively high amount of energy. The most common incandescent light source, the basic bulb the industry calls an ''A bulb,'' is the most wasteful. Typically, it produces less than 20 lumens per watt, compared to 50 or more lumens per watt produced by fluorescent tubes. In addition, the A bulb's allover glow means that it scatters light wastefully, spilling as much light *inside* a lamp as it actually sheds in your room.

Saving energy with incandescents

The easiest way to save energy and still use the relatively inexpensive A bulbs is to look for the newest, high-efficiency ''miser'' designs; check the lumen output printed on the package, and buy the bulb that has the highest lumen/watt ratio. Be aware that you'll save by using one higher-wattage bulb instead of several smaller bulbs, for example, by replacing four 25-watt bulbs in a fix-

ture with one 100-watt bulb. Next, examine the various other types of bulbs available. Replace ordinary bulbs with reflector bulbs, which have silvered backs to direct the light efficiently, and you'll need less wattage. For instance, a 50-watt reflector bulb inside an ordinary pole lamp or canister-style floor lamp will cast a more intense, defined beam of light on your reading material than a higher-wattage A bulb.

Types of bulbs

1. *Long-life A bulbs.* Long-life bulbs cost more than standard bulbs, but they're worth it when you compare their 2,500-hour life expectancy to the 1,000-hour span of ordinary A bulbs. Use long-life bulbs in awkward or hard-to-reach places.
2. *Tubular* or *showcase bulbs.* Tube-shaped bulbs are used in appliances, aquariums, and many decorative fixtures, such as the specialty shelf lights in china cabinets.
3. *Silvered-bowl bulbs.* A silvery coating on the rounded portion of these bulbs reduces glare; use them in hanging, open-bottom lights where bare bulbs shine in your eyes.
4. *Globe* or *G bulbs.* Globe bulbs, available in either clear or white, smoked, colored, and silver, are used most often in decorative fixtures, such as strip lights around mirrors.
5. *Clear A bulbs.* These bulbs also are decorative; they can create a prismatic light effect in glass, crystal, or Tiffany-style lamps and fixtures.
6. *High-intensity bulbs.* These bulbs are popular in desk lamps. They produce more output and intensity in light than wattage indicates.
7. *Reflector* or *R bulbs* . Reflector bulbs are efficient, directing about 85 percent of the light they produce in the

direction you aim it. Use them in directional reading lights or in track fixtures to focus a defined beam on a nearby work of art. *Mini-spot R bulbs* often are used in recessed-eyeball and track-light fixtures, as well as some portable lamps. *Flood R bulbs* produce a wide beam of light to illuminate a wall display; they're also used in some outdoor security fixtures.
8. *Decorative chandelier bulbs*. These bulbs are ideal for chandeliers, sconces, coach lights, and similar fixtures. Some bulbs have the appearance of etched crystal, gaslight, or candlelight.
9. *Quartz halogen*. Low-wattage halogen bulbs are gaining popularity in homes. These high-performance bulbs are useful as task lights and to highlight architectural details and artwork. They produce more lumens per watt than standard bulbs.
10. *Ellipsoidal reflector* or *ER bulbs*. These large, pear-shaped bulbs have a silvered backing that focuses light two inches ahead of the bulb, then spreads the light outward. This design prevents light from becoming trapped inside the fixture. Use ER bulbs in place of floods or regular A bulbs in track fixtures.
11. *Parabolic aluminized-reflector* or *PAR bulbs.* Originally designed to withstand outdoor weather conditions, PAR bulbs are useful indoors because of their variety of beam widths. They produce well-defined, focused beams of light that vary in width, depending on the bulb you select. Personnel at specialty lighting shops can help you select the right PAR bulb for your job.

Fluorescent lighting

Fluorescent light is coming into its own as a residential lighting

tool, and with good reason. A real energy-saver, the typical 40-watt fluorescent tube produces nearly 2,200 lumens; a 40-watt incandescent bulb produces only 450 lumens. Fluorescent tubes, whose inner surfaces are coated with fluorescent material, contain mercury vapor, which emits light when it's hit by electrons from the tube's cathode. Until recently, the light from fluorescent tubes was as cold and scientific as that description. Today's color-corrected fluorescents, however, can produce a warm, yellow light that's aesthetically comparable to incandescents.

In addition to standard tubes, new fluorescent shapes and sizes are becoming more common. You can replace standard incandescent bulbs with round, screw-in fluorescents in both table lamps and ceiling fixtures. Some new reading lamps—typically slim, modern designs—are using mini-size fluorescent tubes.

Types of fluorescent tubes

Fluorescent replacement rings for incandescent fixtures. These circle-shape tubes are affixed to a cone-shape adapter so you can screw them into an ordinary light bulb socket. Since the 22-watt fluorescent ring provides as much light as a regular 75-watt A bulb, you'll save energy. That, plus the estimated 50,000-hour life of fluorescent rings, makes them well worth their $20 cost.
12. *Fluorescent tubes.* Fluorescent tubes come in many lengths, diameters, and colors. Use ordinary cool-white versions in work areas, such as laundry centers and home shops; use more costly deluxe warm-white tubes in areas where the appearance of food and furnishings is especially important.

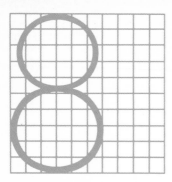
DAYLIGHTING

Many people think using natural light in a decorating plan is a lot like the weather: You can talk about it, but there's nothing much you can do about it. If you're one of those people, this chapter may change your mind. Though you certainly can't make the sun shine, you can control how much sunlight enters your home and orchestrate sunlight's effects on your rooms. We call the process "daylighting"; put simply, it means using the sun to the best advantage at your house.

Too often people enclose their rooms with heavy window treatments that effectively keep out nature's best decorating tool: daylight. If you're one of them, try an experiment: Throw back your curtains and draperies—perhaps even remove them. The change may amaze you.

The homeowners whose bedroom is featured *opposite* wanted the room to have a light, airy feeling. All their decorating choices—even the gauzy fabric hanging from the ceiling—contribute to the breezy atmosphere. The room's most outstanding architectural features are its two unadorned Palladian windows. Left bare and highlighted with a delicate pastel color, they flood the room with daylight, giving it a truly sunny disposi-

tion. Additionally, the absence of curtains fully displays a serene rural view.

Practical considerations

The owners of this home located their bedroom facing south and west to allow late-morning sleeping. Double-glazing makes the windows energy efficient. Privacy isn't a problem here because neighboring houses are distant.

If you need privacy or have an unattractive view, but would like to admit more daylight, consider translucent shades or a skylight. In the narrow bathroom pictured *below*, a fixed skylight opens up the space with a treetop view. A small window below the skylight provides ventilation.

(continued)

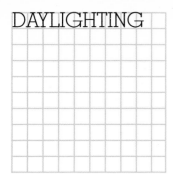

MAKING THE MOST OF NATURAL LIGHT
(continued)

Unadorned windows and skylights are only two ways to welcome the sun into your home. Here are a couple of less conventional approaches: Go big and really open up a room, or search out unusual places to let in light. The rooms shown on these pages demonstrate how each strategy works to give a room its brightest outlook.

Thinking big

As the gallery pictured *opposite* proves, some homeowners aren't faint of heart about admitting natural light. Here, windows line almost the full length and height of the wall. Treating the wall like this permits sunlight to penetrate throughout the long, narrow space; anything less could have created large shadow areas that would visually constrict the room's sense of openness. The double-glazed windows also let all of the stone floor absorb sunlight. Heat stored in the stone is released as the room cools, making the gallery energy efficient.

Creative thinking

To make the most of natural light in the finished attic shown *above,* the homeowners took both a sunny-side-up and a sunny-side-down approach. When planning this family gathering place, they decided on a conventional—and large—skylight for the left side of the room. But they weren't satisfied to leave the skylight as the attic's only daylight source. Ruling out a dormer (it would have interrupted the house's exterior lines), they decided to balance natural light throughout the room by taking an opposite approach to skylighting: They removed soffit material to open up the joists that support a deep roof overhang. This brings indirect light—bounced up from the side of the house and a patio below—into the attic through a glass knee wall. The finished white wall helps reflect light from below into the room. The glass knee wall keeps out the elements and has operable windows to permit the room to let off steam in the summer.

GROWING PLANTS INDOORS

Daylight and plants naturally go together. Let in sunshine and you've let in one of a plant's most important needs. This means that with a little care, you can use newfound light to create a natural indoor setting.

In the garden room pictured *opposite,* the homeowners come as close as possible to dining *alfresco* without going outside. Thanks to a prefab greenhouse added by opening up a kitchen wall, they now have a sunny spot that can be enjoyed year-round. In balmy weather, sliding glass doors on all sides admit breezes.

If you plan a garden room, remember that plants need more than just good light to thrive. They also require proper nutrition, the right amount of water, and warm temperatures—usually 50 to 85 degrees Fahrenheit. In areas that have harsh winters, a garden room usually needs at least some mechanical heating, or a system for storing and releasing solar heat. Otherwise, few plants will survive nighttime temperature drops.

Even if a garden room isn't in your plans, don't forsake houseplants. All you need is a sun-filled spot. The light- and plant-filled corner shown *at right,* for example, adds beauty and visual interest to what once was a dreary bedroom. The boxlike space had just a few windows that only dimly lighted the room. To overcome this architectural shortcoming, the homeowners opened up the roof with a skylight. To amplify the natural light—and to visually expand this corner of the room—they butted two floor-to-ceiling mirrors. Now, the room appears sunny and spacious, and a once-dark corner has become a little piece of paradise.

(continued)

GROWING PLANTS INDOORS
(continued)

HOUSEPLANTS AND THEIR LIGHT NEEDS

CATEGORY	PLANT NAME	NATURAL LIGHT
FLOWERING PLANTS	African violet	bright, indirect
	Begonia	bright, indirect
	Geranium	bright, direct
	Gloxinia	bright, indirect
	Impatiens	bright, indirect
	Mum	bright, indirect
	Primrose	bright, indirect
CACTUS AND OTHER SUCCULENTS	Aloe	bright, direct
	Bunny-ears	bright, direct
	Christmas cactus	bright, indirect
	Cow-tongue cactus	bright, indirect
	Easter-lily cactus	bright, direct
	Fishhook cactus	bright, direct
	Jade plant	bright, direct
FOLIAGE PLANTS	Chinese evergreen	filtered
	Coleus	bright, direct
	Dieffenbachia	filtered
	Grape ivy	bright, indirect
	Peperomia	bright, indirect
	Sansevieria	bright, indirect
	Wandering Jew	bright, indirect
FERNS	Asparagus (myersi)	bright, indirect
	Asparagus (sprengeri)	bright, indirect
	Bird's-nest	bright, indirect
	Boston	bright, indirect
	Hare's-foot	bright, indirect
	Rabbit's-foot	filtered
	Staghorn	bright, indirect
PALMS	Bamboo	bright, indirect
	Butterfly	bright, indirect
	Chinese fan	bright, indirect
	European fan	bright, direct
	Fishtail	bright, indirect
	Miniature date	bright, indirect
	Parlor	bright, indirect
	Sentry	bright, indirect
BROMELIADS	Billbergia	bright, direct
	Earth-star	bright, indirect
	Grecian-vase	bright, indirect
	Guzmania	bright, indirect
	Neoregelia	bright, direct
	Pineapple	bright, direct
	Urn plant	bright, indirect

ARTIFICIAL LIGHT	COMMENTS
14-16 hours daily	Geraniums and begonias are special.
14-16 hours daily	You'll need to experiment before you
14-16 hours daily	find what's right.
14-16 hours daily	
12-16 hours daily	
14-16 hours daily	
14-16 hours daily	
14-16 hours daily	Desert cactus, such as the Bunny-
14-16 hours daily	ears, should be no more than 4 inch-
14-16 hours daily	es from artificial or plant lights. Keep
14-16 hours daily	succulents no more than 6 inches
14-16 hours daily	from artificial light. In sunlight,
14-16 hours daily	use only east, south, and west
14-16 hours daily	exposures.
10-12 hours daily	For fluorescent lighting, place plants
14-16 hours daily	6-12 inches below lights. If using in-
12-14 hours daily	candescent light, keep plants 18-24
10-12 hours daily	inches below lights.
14-16 hours daily	
12-14 hours daily	
14-16 hours daily	
10-12 hours daily	Place 8-12 inches below artificial
10-12 hours daily	lights. Be careful not to burn under
14-16 hours daily	lights. Never expose to direct sun-
12-14 hours daily	light. Use a sheer curtain if neces-
14-16 hours daily	sary to filter light.
12-14 hours daily	
14-16 hours daily	
12-14 hours daily	Palms like plenty of light and water,
14-16 hours daily	but use porous soil and don't let
14-16 hours daily	pots stand in water. Bamboo and
14-16 hours daily	parlor palms prefer lower light and
14-16 hours daily	less water. Feed with slow-release
14-16 hours daily	houseplant food.
12-16 hours daily	
14-16 hours daily	
14-16 hours daily	Exotic but almost foolproof plants.
14-16 hours daily	Prefer bright sun, but tolerate poor
14-16 hours daily	light. Direct sun burns leaves; a
14-16 hours daily	sunny east or west window is more
12-16 hours daily	suitable. The stiffer a plant's leaves,
14-16 hours daily	the more light it needs. Keep water
14-16 hours daily	in plant's center cup.

To put your houseplants in the limelight, you must first put them in the right light. The trick is to know how much light is available, then choose the best plants for that level of light. Once you do that—and take care of a few other plant needs—you're on the way to a thriving bit-of-the-tropics in your home.

Natural light

In indoor gardening literature, you'll often see terms like "full sunlight," "bright, direct light," "bright, indirect light," or "filtered or medium light." These are terms plant experts use to help you find the right plant for the right spot in your home.

• *Full sunlight* means just that: sun shining directly on a plant throughout most of the day, usually from a south-facing window. This light is too strong for most plants. You can filter the light with a sheer curtain or drapery.

• *Bright, direct light* is less intense than full sunlight. To achieve this, place plants in a southeast, southwest, or west exposure or a few feet away from a south window. Schefflera and coleus are a couple of plants that require this light level.

• *Bright, indirect light* is reflected light—usually from white walls. The intensity of this light is roughly equivalent to east or west sun. This is the kind of light most foliage plants need.

• *Filtered or medium light* is strong enough to read by. A northern exposure gives medium light—perfect for snake plant, English ivy, and Chinese evergreen. It's roughly equivalent to light a few feet away from an east or west window.

Artificial light

If sunlight is in short supply in your home, consider artificial lights for your houseplants.

Sunlight contains all the wavelengths of the visible spectrum. Out of this full spectrum, plants use blue wavelengths to develop foliage, and the red end of the spectrum to produce blossoms.

You may have noticed that houseplants fare poorly under ordinary household lights. That's because incandescent lights are strong in the red end of the spectrum but lack blue wavelengths, and typical "cool-white" fluorescents produce plenty of blue light, but are short on red.

One solution often employed by commercial growers is to combine incandescent with fluorescent light sources. An easier alternative for home growers is to use plant lights— specially engineered incandescent bulbs and fluorescent tubes that produce the blue and red portions of the light spectrum that plants need. By using plant lights you can achieve the same light levels artificially as are possible naturally.

With plant lights, the key factors are the distance you situate plants from the lights and the amount of time the plant lights are on. Locate plants that require bright, direct sunlight no more than 7 inches from the lights; to reproduce filtered, medium light, locate plants up to 32 inches away. Most plants need 14 to 16 hours of light per day. If plants aren't doing well under lights, move them closer or leave the lights on for longer periods. With an inexpensive timer you can program the lights to operate automatically.

For best results (and a reputation for having a green thumb), use the chart *at left* to help you accurately select the plants best for your room's sunny spots.

TREATING WINDOWS WISELY

Too much of a good thing—even natural daylight—can spoil the effect you seek. So, before you rush to strip away window treatments at your house, be sure to consider a room's exposure and its function.

A room with a southern exposure ushers in bright light most of the day. A north-facing room, on the other hand, receives less intense, but more even light. In general, daytime rooms function best with a southern or eastern exposure; evening and nighttime rooms work well with northern and western exposures.

To regulate daylight and give a room the atmosphere you want, you have two choices: Control light from the outside or from the inside.

One indoor solution

The wall of windows in the living/dining room pictured *at right* posed a problem for the house's owners. They wanted the room to maximize daylighting without compromising privacy. Additionally, they sought a window treatment that would show off the windows' stair-step molding, and emphasize the room's strong design lines. Their choice: mini-slat blinds.

With most mini-slat blinds, a simple turn of a wand offers seemingly magical control. Completely open, the blinds let in nearly as much light as a bare window would. Tilted up, they deflect light to the upper parts of a room, creating softness; tilted down, they throw light to the floor, giving a room greater visual depth. Fully closed, they provide complete privacy.

Other indoor controls

Mini-slat blinds are just one answer to controlling natural light from the inside. If instead of a tailored look you prefer window treatments that cast a romantic spell, try lace curtains or matchstick blinds. Lace filters streaming sunlight to sprinkle soft shadows throughout a room. And matchstick blinds, more casual in nature, warm a room by giving daylight a perpetually rosy look.

Wooden shutters are another flexible way to control light, especially if you use the typical treatment of four shutters to a window. Fold open all of the shutters for maximum brightness. For good light with adequate privacy, open the top shutters and keep the bottom ones fully closed. For filtered light, leave all shutters closed, but tilt their movable louvers to admit just the right amount of light.

Going outside for help

If controlling light from the inside doesn't work for you, it's time for outside help. Here again, you have plenty of options to select from, starting with updated versions of the old-fashioned awning. Some of today's awnings are a far cry from yesteryear's in appearance and modus operandi, but all have the same purpose: to protect a room from too much direct sunlight and the heat that comes with it. Adjustable awnings let you fine-tune the amount of light you want. Fixed "hood" awnings offer less flexibility, but still shield out the sun's hottest rays.

Other exterior shading systems include roll-up shutters, solar screens, and louvers. They, and the treatments described on the next two pages, help control natural light and save energy.

(continued)

TREATING WINDOWS WISELY

(continued)

When you let natural light into your home, make sure you don't let heated or cooled air out. You'll find it hard to enjoy a sunny room if you know you're wasting energy dollars.

Being energy-wise doesn't mean holing yourself up in a totally enclosed room, however. In the room shown on pages 122 and 123, for example, the window treatment is no treatment at all. Double-glazing makes the room beautiful, yet miserly.

Two more energy-smart daylighting ideas are shown here. In the dining area pictured *at left,* vertical blinds reveal a split personality—all to a homeowner's energy advantage. In winter, the blinds can open like traverse draperies to give the room a blast of welcome sunshine and its accompanying heat. In summer, they help control the sun's blazing rays by rotating to let in as much (or as little) sun as you wish. The result: A room that's toasty in winter and adopts a cooler personality for summer.

The dining area pictured *opposite* also is energy conscious. Quilted shades roll up and down in tracks to control natural light and air leaks. Backing the shades is a foil lining that saves energy in two ways. The foil reflects summer's sun to keep out heat; on winter nights it acts as a second layer of insulation to keep heat in. The quilting also works doubly hard. Besides being a good insulator, it provides psychological warmth. Even in winter's worst weather, this alcove feels snug and warm.

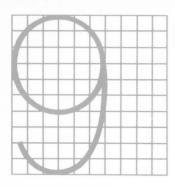

LIGHTING PROJECTS

Constructing your own lamps and fixtures can be both financially and aesthetically rewarding—and you don't have to be a wiring wizard or creative genius to do it. This chapter guides you through the construction of more than half a dozen intriguing projects and lights the way for many more ideas.

BOXED-IN LIGHTING

Boxed-in lighting provides subtle illumination with style and flexibility. The cornice lighting pictured *at right,* mounted at the intersection of the wall and ceiling, is just one type. Here, the designer wanted to accent the simple white walls and emphasize the conservatively contemporary decor. Mounting lights behind the painted cornice achieved this effect with minimal expense and effort.

The cornice itself is a simple box; pieces of 1x12 lumber shield incandescent reflector lamps mounted inside. Here the lamps are screwed into track fixtures; if you don't need the flexibility, you can save money by using a series of simple porcelain sockets.

Another alternative is to use fluorescent tubes inside; in most settings you'll probably prefer the light provided by warm white fluorescents to that cast by cool whites.

Whatever type of lighting you select, paint the inside of the cornice white for maximum light reflectance. The outside color or covering is up to you. The cornice pictured here was covered with drywall for a built-in look, then painted to blend with the walls. Plain lumber also could be painted or stained to match or contrast with the walls.

Cornices aren't the only ways to box in light fixtures. Valances, for instance, are mounted lower on the wall than cornices—often above draperies—to shed both up- and downlight. The tube or bulb is shielded only on the sides. Cove lighting provides dramatic uplight on a ceiling. With cove lighting, the tube or bulb is shielded at the bottom and sides. For more about these and other types of built-in lighting, see pages 116–117.

LIGHTING STAIRS AND HALLWAYS

Hallways don't have to be dull—or dim—and stairways never should be. Installing the right kind and amount of lighting in these vital transitional areas is a matter of safety as well as appearance. Well-chosen lighting can enlarge a small hall, dramatize an interesting-ly shaped stairwell, and minimize the danger of painful falls. Here are two examples of home-grown lighting arrange-ments that accomplish all that.

A distinctive architectural element in its own right, the hallway pictured *opposite* commands additional attention thanks to innovative lighting. Here, the high ceiling was dropped around a ply-wood frame and painted black to visually alter the hall's long, narrow dimensions. Eyeball spotlights set into the sides of the frame call attention to the ceiling treatment. The result: an appealing blend of color, texture, and pattern, plus ample light along the entire length of the hall.

The subtly yet effectively lit stairway shown *above* also combines decorative impact with creative lighting. Low-level tread-side illumination comes from small fluorescent tubes mounted in a pocket tucked into the underside of the stair-way's banister wall. Additional lighting, not shown here but necessary for overall illumina-tion and safety, is mounted on the ceilings of the upper and lower landings.

When you plan stairway lighting, keep in mind that good light does not mean glare. Usually, wall- or ceiling-mounted fixtures do the job well; if you have an angled stairway, you may want to in-stall a fixture on the middle landing as well as the top and bottom ones. Low-voltage di-rectional lights mounted along the stair rungs at each tread are good safety features. And be sure to put easy-to-reach three-way switches where they can be turned on *before* someone starts to ascend or descend the stairs.

ASSEMBLING YOUR OWN FIXTURES

Lighting that costs less isn't necessarily lighting that delivers less fashion flair. By choosing from a wide variety of lamps, shades, and wiring systems, you can assemble your own high-style fixtures with the look you want at a price you can afford. The only limits are safety and common sense—you must meet electrical code standards and keep within the manufacturer's recommended wattages. On these pages we'll show you two examples of do-it-yourself lighting units that look more costly and complicated than they are.

The home-assembled high-tech track lighting system pictured *above* consists of nothing more than two yellow-enamel clamp lights and a square metal shower rod. Clamp lights come in other colors, too, as well as shiny unpainted metal.

To custom-size this system, the 1-inch-thick rod was cut to fit a 60-inch-long frame. The frame, made of 1x4 pine, is an open box with a back and two sides. Thanks to the box, this type of system can be mounted on any flat surface, horizontally or vertically, and its length can be sized to meet your own needs.

The pretty Victorian-look ceiling fixtures shown *opposite* are far removed stylistically from the innovative track system, but they're just as simple to put together.

Reproduction glass shades such as these are widely available at lighting stores; you also may be able to find second-hand originals. A cord connects the fixture's socket or bulb holder to a ceiling electrical box.

Be sure to use a bulb holder that is UL-approved and wire it with high-temperature conductors. After turning off electricity to the circuit, connect the hot and neutral wires to the ceiling box; below, tie the cord in an Underwriters knot (pictured in the diagram at right), and attach the ends to the fixture socket terminals. For more about wiring fixtures safely, see pages 142 and 143.

HANGING CEILING FIXTURES

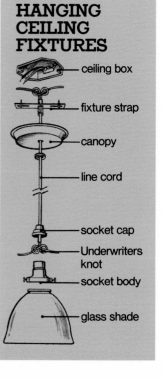

ceiling box

fixture strap

canopy

line cord

socket cap

Underwriters knot

socket body

glass shade

LIGHTING
PROJECTS

ASSEMBLING
YOUR OWN
LAMPS

Why settle for cut-and-dried lighting when you can create your own lamps from whatever lights your imagination? Almost anything can be transformed into a lamp base; old vases, antique jars and bottles, near-antique brass fire extinguishers, and scrap metal or lumber are just the beginning.

The elegant tube-base lamp pictured *opposite* actually is a cluster of chrome-plated shower rod pieces. Cut in a variety of lengths, the 1-inch-diameter rods provide both vertical support and visual interest.

To make this model, the rods were cut into one 24-inch segment and into two 12-inch, two 14-inch, two 16-inch, and two 18-inch segments. You can adjust the lengths to suit your own plans, of course.

Once the rods are cut to size, center the tallest one and arrange the others around it, keeping the bottom ends even. Glue the rods together with epoxy and let them dry.

The base was cut from a 2-inch-thick pine board; again, you could choose another wood or thickness, and cut it to the dimensions you want. Trace an outline of the rod cluster in the center of the board and chisel out ¼ inch of stock.

Directly beneath the longest tube, drill a hole, and then chisel a channel across the bottom of the base to accommodate the cord. Use threaded lamp rod to secure the longest tube and assemble the lamp as shown on pages 142 and 143.

A woodworker's special

The display lamp pictured *above* and in exploded view *above, right* calls for some tricky joinery, but requires no special wiring skills.

Our version was cut from 1x12 cedar. First lay out and cut the side pieces. Next, miter the cut pieces for the front, top, and back. Carefully grove edges of the front and one top piece so you can slide in the square of translucent plastic that shields the bulb.

Before you assemble the lamp, screw a wired ceramic socket to the top rear. Glue ¼x¼-inch wood strips ¾ inch from the bottom edges of the lamp housing; these will hold the bottom piece. Slide the plastic into place and glue and clamp all the wood pieces except the bottom. Next, drill a hole in the side of the lamp for the cord and install the cord and switch. Put a mini-spot bulb in the socket and screw the bottom piece into place.

WIRING LAMPS AND FIXTURES

WIRING A TABLE LAMP

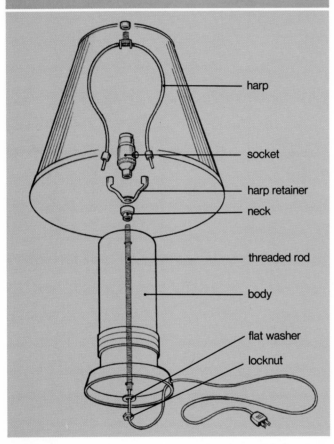

harp

socket

harp retainer

neck

threaded rod

body

flat washer

locknut

WIRING A SWAG LAMP

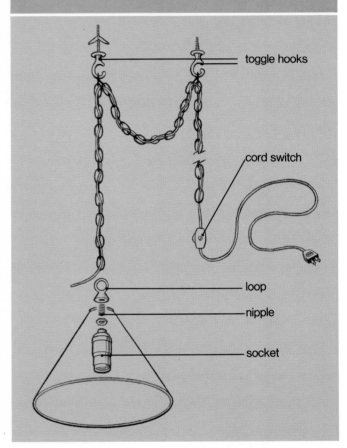

toggle hooks

cord switch

loop

nipple

socket

The general principles of making lamps are fairly straightforward. Almost anything that's hollow will do for the lamp body, and the necessary electrical parts are available at most lamp and lighting stores.

Table lamps

The drawing *above, left* shows the basic workings of a standard table lamp. To assemble a lamp of this general style, you'll need a body (and possibly a base to support the body) and a harp to support the shade. Both screw-on and spring-style harps are available. The working electrical

components consist of a plug, cord, socket, and a threaded rod through which the cord runs inside the lamp body.

To wire a lamp, run the rod up through the body and thread the cord through it. If the lamp body is tall, you may need to stiffen the cord with wire before you can get it through the rod. Secure the rod at the bottom with a locknut washer or two lamp nuts; at the top, use a decorative knurled nut or threaded neck to hold the rod in place. Put a harp retainer over the rod and screw in a socket base.

Next, tie an Underwriters knot, as shown *opposite, up-*

per left. Then strip away the insulation from the end of the cord and attach the cord leads to the proper socket terminals as shown *opposite, lower left*. Attach the plug to the opposite end and reassemble the socket and install the harp. Add a bulb and shade, and you've finished the project.

Hanging lamps

To assemble a hanging lamp, as shown *above, right,* you'll need chain and cord, both of which are available by the running foot in a variety of colors and finishes at most lighting supply stores. The chain usually attaches to the fixture itself

by means of a metal loop. You can attach the loop to the chain by spreading open one of the chain's links, then crimp the link with slip-joint pliers when you're done.

Now thread the loop onto a nipple and screw it to a socket base, as shown *above, right.* Tie an Underwriters knot, strip ¾ inch of insulation from each cord wire, and secure the cord to the socket body. Hang the lamp with toggle or screw hangers. You can use a cord or pull switch to control the light. Be sure the cord doesn't get in the way of traffic or block the view of a nice piece of furniture.

WIRING CLOSE-UPS

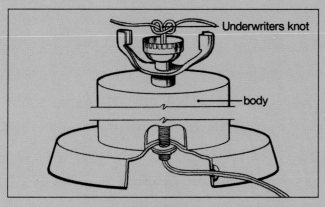

Underwriters knot

body

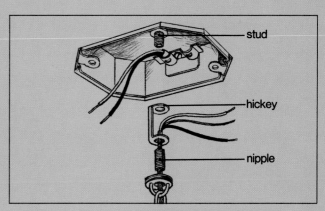

stud

hickey

nipple

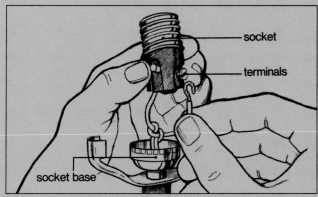

socket

terminals

socket base

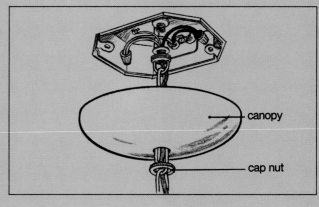

canopy

cap nut

U nless you live in an old-er home with antiquated or unconventional wir-ing and support systems that aren't compatible with more contemporary units, replacing a ceiling fixture with a new one is a fairly simple matter.

Before you remove the old fixture, shut off power to it. Then figure out how the old fix-ture is attached: Some are at-tached to the ceiling as well as the electrical box. Several methods are used, including straps that attach the fixture to bolts (not shown); a hickey that attaches the fixture to a stud in the center of the box, as shown *above, top right*; and

systems that combine features of both.

Once you understand the old fixture, remove the screws or locknuts that hold its cano-py in place. Disconnect the black and white leads, but first take careful note of how they are attached to the old fixture.

Next, read the instructions for mounting the new fixture. Strip about ¾ inch of insula-tion from its leads. If they are stranded, twist the ends slightly.

If the new fixture is heavy, it may need support during the hanging process; use a coat hanger or strong cord for this

purpose. Preassemble as many components as you can to keep the temporary suspen-sion time to a minimum.

If you plan to hang the lamp with a hickey, be sure that all wires exit through the side of the hickey, as shown. Then screw a nipple into the hickey and thread the hickey into the stud. You also could use a strap or metal plate; in fact, you'll need to if the holes in the fixture's canopy don't match those in the box or the box has no center stud to which you can attach a hickey.

Once the fixture is secured physically, it's time to make the electrical connections.

More about this on pages 148–151. Secure the wires with sol-derless connectors or cone-shape wire nuts. Then coil the wires up carefully inside the housing box, as shown *above, lower right*.

Install the light bulbs, then screw or bolt the lamp fixture to the wall or ceiling. Turn on the current. If the light doesn't work, make sure the bulb is in-stalled properly. If the bulb isn't the problem, turn off the current again and take the fix-ture apart. Be sure that con-nections are not crossed or out of contact, and be sure all points of connection are prop-erly insulated.

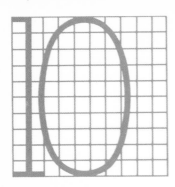

WIRING AND SWITCHING BASICS

Wiring new fixtures, and the switches that control them, may seem intimidating at first, but compared to other around-the-house jobs, electrical projects go together fairly quickly. The components are highly modular, which takes a lot of the guesswork out of assembling them; it's difficult in many cases to install something upside down or backward—even the wires are color-coded. This chapter shows how to install new wires without turning your home inside out, how to wire electrical boxes to provide power to new switches and light fixtures, how to put up track lighting systems, and how to use energy-efficient fluorescent fixtures when installing luminous ceilings.

FISHING WIRES

The toughest part of supplementing or altering your home's electrical system is not wiring the switches, outlets, and fixtures themselves, but figuring out how to weave new electrical cable behind walls, under floors, and over ceilings to the points where you need power.

Once you've found a likely route, the next step is to clear a path for the cable to follow. Along the way, you'll probably run into a 2x4 plate at the bottom of each wall, a double 2x4 plate at the top, and maybe a 2x4 fireblock at the midpoint between plates. If you can get at a wall from above or below, you can drill through plates with a brace and a long bit; if not, chisel out a channel, as shown on the opposite page, then patch the surface later.

Once you've established a route for the cable, you're ready for a fishing expedition. Instead of a rod and reel, though, you'll probably want to use a fish tape, a thin, springy metal band that's fed into and through places your hands (and your eyes) can't reach.

The tape, which will eventually reel in the new electrical cable, will almost certainly encounter obstacles along the way. But this is where patience and perseverance pay off, so keep at it until the tape reappears at the desired location. After the tape has blazed the trail, neatly tape the new electrical cable to it and reverse the process, slowly pulling the cable back along the same route.

Naturally, once the cable is in place and the new switches, outlets, and fixtures have been wired, you'll face some repair jobs. To minimize post-wiring restoration requirements, make every effort to do as little damage as possible along the way. Running a new cable behind the ceiling molding, baseboards, or the woodwork around a door frame can drastically reduce the amount of wall patching you'll have to do after the wiring is completed.

WORKING TO CODE

Both the electrical materials you use and the way they are to be installed are mandated by law. The law is based upon the National Electrical Code (NEC), which is published by the National Fire Protection Association, a nonprofit agency.

The NEC is a compendium of rules, regulations, and standards that covers almost every electrical situation. Chances are, your local bookstore or city building department will have copies of this code; you'll also be able to find copies of your official codes at the library and municipal building.

Check with building department officials to find out if you need a permit to extend an existing circuit or add a new one, and whether you'll need a licensed electrician to do the final hookup.

If you ignore the statutes you may have to pay a fine as well as pay for the work to be redone; more important, improper installation could jeopardize your home and the safety of those who live there.

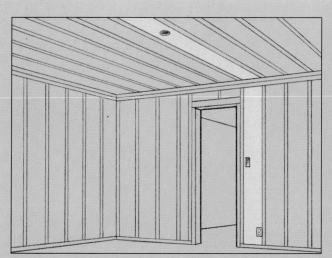

1 Getting electrical cable to a new ceiling fixture takes more patience and planning than skill. First, determine which way the ceiling joists run; that's the route the cable will have to follow. Cut an opening for the fixture in line with the new opening for the wall switch. To make getting power to the new switch easier, try to locate the switch in the same wall cavity as an existing receptacle.

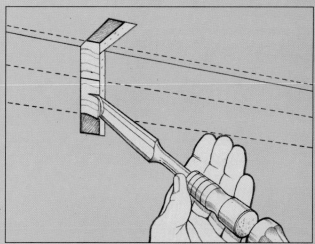

2 Where the wall and the ceiling come together, make ¾x4-inch openings. Next, chisel a channel in the 2x4 plates behind the drywall or plaster. The channel will later serve as a recessed path for the electrical cable.

After the wiring is in place, you can fill in openings with plaster or patching compound. If there is ceiling molding in the room, you may be able to hide your work behind it.

3 Slowly feed a springy metal fish tape into the ceiling. Aim for the opening you've made for the fixture. Chances are, you'll have to advance and retreat the tape several times. When the end of the tape reaches the fixture opening, attach the electrical cable to the end. Then reverse the process, pulling the cable into the ceiling and back to the channel opening.

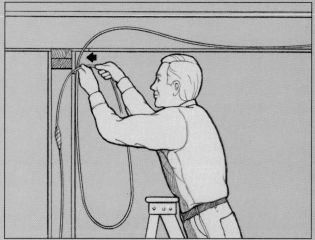

4 Finally, feed the cable down through the wall to the switch box opening (or use the fish tape again). Now the cable runs from the ceiling fixture to the switch. To get power to the switch box, feed another length of cable from the switch box opening to the receptacle below. After the receptacle, switch, and fixture box have been wired, staple the cable into the channel in the plates and repair the wall.

INSTALLING BOXES

If you're installing electrical boxes in unfinished spaces, the standard practice is to attach them to the wall studs and ceiling joists. But without excavating big holes, how do you get at these structural elements when they've already been covered by drywall or plaster? In most cases, you don't have to.

Ordinarily, retrofitting a new switch, receptacle, or fixture requires only that you cut a hole in the wall or ceiling the same size as the new electrical box. Electrical parts manufacturers have simplified the actual installation process by making boxes and accessories that fasten to the insides of walls and ceilings.

There are dozens of different boxes on the market to suit your particular needs. Ask a hardware clerk to recommend the appropriate box for the kind of surface you'll be dealing with (paneling, drywall, or lath and plaster) and the type of cable (armored or sheathed) you'll be using.

If possible, choose a box with internal cable clamps—so you won't have to bother with special connectors to hook up the wires—and one that adjusts to differing wall thicknesses. Most boxes are designed to be "gangable," which means you can remove a side plate from each and join them together to accommodate two switches, two receptacles, or one of each in a side-by-side arrangement. Here are the general types of boxes you'll encounter.

• *Switch/receptacle boxes* hold either device and serve as the workhorses in any electrical installation. They measure 3x2 inches and come in a variety of depths. (More about this below.)

• *Nonmetallic switch/receptacle boxes* are made of plastic

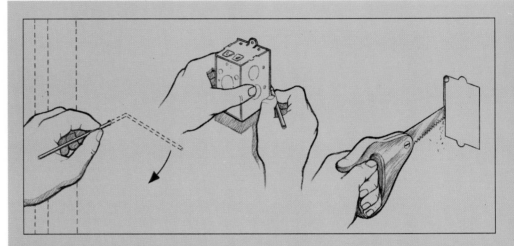

To find a location for an electrical box, drill a test hole in the wall, insert a bent wire, and rotate it. If the wire makes a circle, you've found a good site. If it hits something, move a few inches away and try again.

Some boxes made for use in finished spaces come with templates that can be placed against the surface and traced around. You also can use the box itself. Center it over the test hole, level, and outline the box.

Now, follow the outline to make an opening for the box. Apply masking tape around the outline to prevent edges from crumbling.Use a utility knife if the surface is drywall. For paneled or plaster-and-lath surfaces, use a keyhole saw.

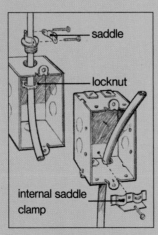

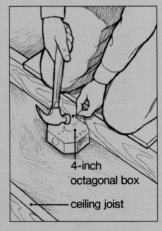

Boxes also differ in the method used to attach the cable inside. One popular model employs an above-the-box saddle and an internal locknut. However, a single-screw, internal saddle-clamp box has fewer parts and is easier to assemble.

Because a ceiling box has to support the weight of a light fixture, it should be fastened to a ceiling joist. If you've planned in advance to secure the box to a joist accessible in the attic, nail an L-bracket box to the wood.

If your ceiling fixture box has to be positioned between the joists, suspend the box on a bar hanger that can be installed on the attic side of the ceiling. Or you can make your own bar hanger out of a 2x4 toe-nailed at each end into the joists.

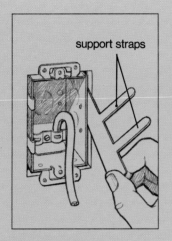

support straps

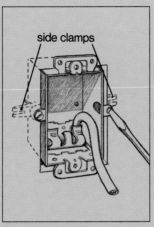

side clamps

spring clips

Once you've cut the box opening and fished and fastened the cable, install one of several kinds of boxes. Boxes with metal support straps are particularly good for securing switch/receptacle boxes to gypsum walls or plaster-and-lath surfaces.

Two-screw side-clamp boxes grip the wall from behind when the screws are tightened, keeping the front of the box flush with the surface. Be sure to select the right size box for the wall thickness you'll be dealing with.

Designed for use with drywall surfaces, some plastic boxes use two spring clips to keep the switch or receptacle box in place. Once the cable has been clamped inside, push the box into the cavity and the clips pop out on the inside of the wall.

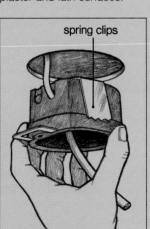

spring clips

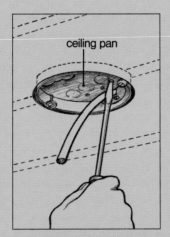

ceiling pan

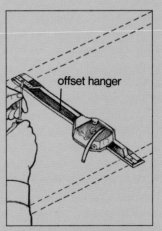

offset hanger

If you don't have access to the attic, you have several options for installing a ceiling fixture. One is to use a spring clip fixture box. Trace around it, cut the hole, thread the cable into the box, and gently push the box into the cavity.

A ceiling pan box, which requires a recess in the ceiling of only ½ inch, is a convenient alternative if you can screw the box directly into a joist. A disadvantage is that fishing the wire through may be more difficult.

If you're dealing with a no-attic-access plaster ceiling, use an offset hanger. Chip out a channel and a cavity for the box, secure the box to the hanger, thread the cable into the box, and screw the ends of the hanger to the joists. Then replaster.

and are prohibited by some codes. They can't be ganged.
• *Fixture/junction boxes* support lighting fixtures or split circuits off into separate branches. They measure 4x4 inches, with a variety of depths, and come in octagonal, round, or square shapes.
• *Utility* or *handy boxes* have the same dimensions as conventional switch/receptacle and fixture/junction boxes, but they have rounded corners. Use utility boxes only in exposed locations. They can't be ganged.
• *Weatherproof boxes* are used outside. They look much like the ones used inside, but are heftier and have gaskets, waterproof covers, and rubber-sealed connections. Weatherproof boxes can't be ganged.

When you're selecting boxes, bear in mind that codes typically specify the number of connections and electrical devices permitted in a particular box. If your installation will exceed these maximums, ask for an extra-deep box.

Connecting cables
Just before you install any box, you have to securely connect a cable or cables to it. Here are the main types of cable connectors.
• *Internal saddle clamps,* shown on the opposite page, let you capture the cable by simply turning a screw inside the box. Always feed about six inches of cable into the box before clamping it.
• *Clamp connectors,* also shown opposite, use a similar device on the outside of the box.
• *Plastic connectors* can be used either inside or outside a box. Pop the connector into a hole, feed cable through it, and then tighten a capture screw.

WIRING SWITCHES AND FIXTURES

After you've fished cable and installed electrical boxes, the next step toward expanding your electrical system is to wire the switches and fixtures together to create a new circuit. Before you start the process, consider the following points.

In most cases you'll probably be using two-wire cable. Actually, there are three wires you'll be dealing with: a black current-carrying (or "hot") wire; a white neutral wire; and a green, green and yellow, or bare grounding wire, which prevents potentially hazardous short circuits. This standardized color-coding system helps take the guesswork out of determining which wire goes on which terminal.

Sometimes, particularly in three-way switch installations, you'll need a three-wire cable, which really has four wires—the three mentioned above and a fourth, red "traveler" wire that runs between each of the switches but bypasses the fixture itself. Read more about three-way switches on pages 150 and 151.

As you'll see in the illustrations on this and the following pages, the white neutral wire sometimes behaves like a black or red "hot" wire in order to complete the circuit. When this happens, mark the white wire with black paint or black tape at each end to remind yourself and anyone else doing electrical work in your home that the wire now is carrying an electrical charge.

You'll also notice in the examples that follow that the way a switch and fixture are wired is partly determined by where they are located in relation to the power source. In some installations, the power will flow to and through the switch to the fixture; in others it will flow to and through the fixture to the switch. Determine in advance the power flow in the installation you're considering before you start work, then plan the wiring process accordingly.

In any switch-and-fixture installation, hooking up the ground wires first will get them out of your way and help reduce confusion.

Making connections
One final, important thing to realize about switches is that they interrupt only the hot leg of the circuit. This means that you connect to them only black, red, or black-painted white wires. White neutral wires that pass through a switch box should be connected only to each other and not to any switch terminal.

Wiring fixtures is straightforward: You connect the fixture's black lead to a current-carrying wire, its white to a neutral. To learn about installing and securing fixtures, see pages 142 and 143.

Make all connections by baring about ¾ inch of wire. At switches, wrap the wire clockwise around a screw terminal. Connect wires by holding them parallel and screwing on a wire nut.

Since you'll have to start work at a junction box, switch, or receptacle that is already electrified, go to the home's main electrical service panel and shut off the power to that particular circuit, or shut down the entire system by tripping the main circuit breaker. It's wise to invest a few dollars in a neon test light, which can tell you which wires are "live." After properly using the test light, you can shut off power to an individual circuit and leave the power running in the remainder of the house.

(continued)

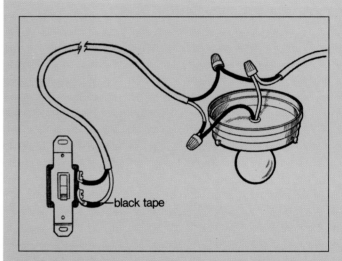

black tape

1 Sometimes you have to make an exception to the color rules. Here, the white wire between switch and fixture is marked with black tape to show that it, too, is hot. In other words, it acts like a black wire. Because the source feed's black and white wires are committed to a black from the switch and a white from the fixture, the remaining white wire from the switch has to go to the fixture's black wire.

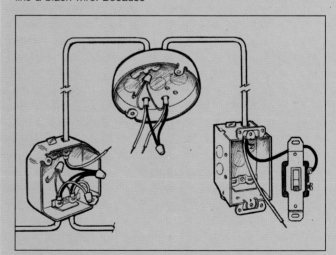

4 In this installation, power flows from the junction box to and through the fixture box and on to the switch via the black wire. Use plastic wire nuts to connect the black wires together as shown. Connect the three black wires in the junction box and the two black wires in the fixture box. Follow the same procedure to connect the ground wires.

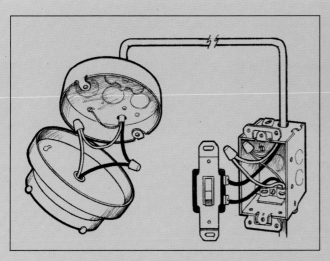

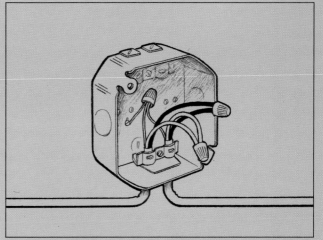

2 Here, power first goes to the switch and then to the fixture. Since the switch interrupts only the circuit's hot leg, there's no need to connect the white wires to it. Instead, attach the white wires to each other as shown. Hook the black wire from the power source to one switch terminal. Hook the black wire leading to the fixture to the other switch terminal. Inside the fixture box, attach the black wires together.

3 Junction boxes are electrical intersections where various circuits come together. Locate the junction box that's nearest to your new switch or fixture and, if possible, run the new cable to or from this point. To find the circuit you want—the one that powers a receptacle in the same room, for example—test the various sets of wires one by one with a continuity tester.

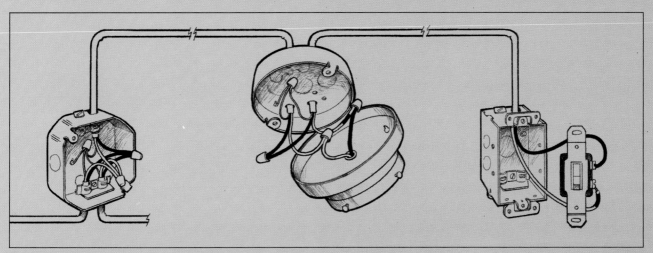

5 With the ground wires and current-carrying black wires properly connected, all that remains to complete the new circuit is to deal with the remaining white wires. Mark the white wire running between the fixture box and the switch with black tape. Hook one end of it to the bottom terminal on the switch. Connect the other end of the black-taped white wire to the black fixture lead. The white wire inside the fixture box then needs to be connected to the light fixture's white lead. Back at the junction box, the white wire from your new cable needs to be connected to the two other white wires. Got all that straight? If not, don't feel alone. It takes a while to get the hang of switch installations, and even electricians sometimes goof.

WIRING SWITCHES AND FIXTURES
(continued)

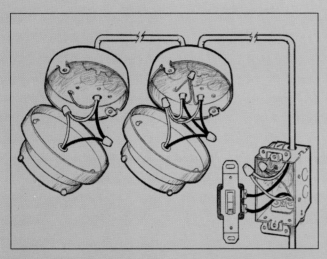

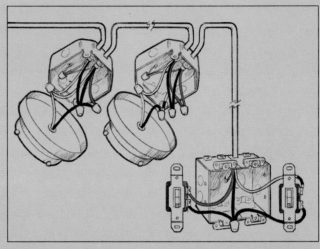

1 Power goes to the switch first, but this time to *two* fixtures. Here, the various wires mate only with wires of the same color. Connect ground wires as shown. At the switch box, connect both black wires to the terminals.

At the first fixture box, attach three black wires to each other and three white wires to each other. At the second fixture box, it's two blacks and two whites.

2 Here, a two-conductor cable feeds power to the left fixture first; three-conductor cable runs between and on to two switches, each controlling one light. Again, get the ground wires out of the way first, connecting

them as shown. Then, following the illustration, move on to the black, red, and white wires. Code the white wires with black tape again to show that they are hot.

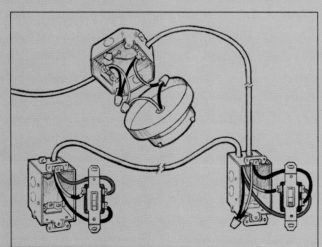

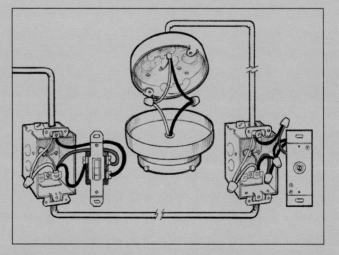

4 Here the power goes to the fixture, then to both three-way switches. Three-conductor cable runs between switches only. Attach the ceiling outlet's hot wire to the common screw of the first switch. Connect red and

white travelers (tape whites) as shown. Connect the black wire from the three-conductor cable to the common screw on the second switch and to the white wire on the first switch (tape it, too).

5 Here's a situation where one three-way switch is a dimmer. In this case, power comes in through the toggle switch, flows to the dimmer, then to the fixture. Again, three-conductor cable is required between switches.

As before, the incoming hot leg goes to the first switch's common screw and red and black travelers run between switches.

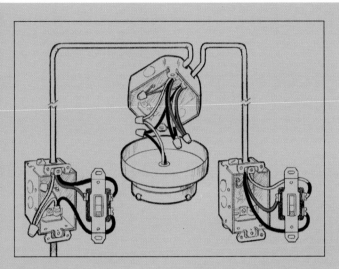

3 To control one fixture from two switches in different locations, you need three-way switches. This and the two following cases show three ways to hook them up, depending on the arrangement of switches, power source, and fixture. Here, the power route is switch-fixture-switch.

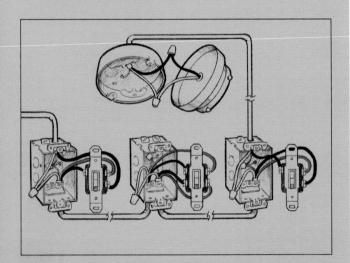

6 Four-way switches, which have four terminals, can control a light from three or more locations. But the first and last switches on line must be three-ways. Again, the power source's black wire goes to the first switch's common pole. Then connect switch-to-switch travelers as shown. Link the second switch's black pole to the fixture's black lead to complete the hot leg. Finally, connect all whites back to the power source.

ow we're going to consider controlling a fixture or fixtures with two or more switches. This is only slightly more involved than the illustrations on the preceding two pages. The switch-and-fixture installations shown here allow you to customize your electrical system to suit your particular lighting needs by allowing you to activate two lights from one location or one light from several locations (at the top and bottom of stairs, for example).

In the first installation shown, standard two-conductor cable is used. But in the other five cases, three-conductor cable is required to complete the circuit. Once again, note that the ordinarily neutral white wire takes on the characteristics of a black wire in some cases, carrying a charge from the switch to the fixture box or vice versa. When that becomes necessary, don't forget to use black tape or paint to indicate that the white wire is now hot.

As before, the wiring procedure is partly determined by the power route, that is, whether the electricity flows from the switch to the fixture or from the fixture to the switch.

The trickiest thing about three- and four-way switches isn't the wiring itself, but the terminology. A three-way switch, for example, controls lights from two locations and has three terminals or poles, a dark-colored one for the "common wire" and two light-colored ones for the "traveler" wires. Three basic rules apply here: Always attach the incoming black hot wire to the common terminal on one switch; always run a hot wire (black or black-marked white) from the common terminal on the sec-

ond switch to the black wire on the fixture; always connect the two traveler terminals of one switch to the traveler terminals on the other switch.

As always, if you hook up all the grounding wires first, you'll contend with fewer loose ends. And of course, be sure to shut off the power before you begin connecting any wires.

Dimmer switches
A mood-setting dimmer switch can be substituted for any one of the standard flip switches anywhere along the line in most multiple-switch installations. Once reserved for theatrical lighting, the dimmer switch is fast becoming a staple in American homes. And no wonder: It gives you fingertip control of the amount of light you want, from candleglow low to spotlight-bright.

Three-way dimmers, pictured in example 5, have hot lead wires rather than ordinary terminals. Because they're expensive and fairly delicate, it's crucial to hook dimmers up right the first time; otherwise, you run the risk of burning them out.

If the directions that come with the dimmer are foggy, it may be worth the trouble to install a standard three-pole toggle switch first as a test. If it functions properly when the power is restored, cut the power again and transfer the wires, one at a time, to the dimmer. Be sure to note the wattage limitations (usually 600 or 1,500) on the dimmer you have selected.

INSTALLING TRACK LIGHTING

A track lighting system may have any number of individual lights, but it's really just one elongated fixture that requires a single electrical box recessed into the ceiling. For that reason alone, installing a track lighting system with, say, six integral lights is far easier than installing six individual fixtures. The surface-mounted track with the wiring inside eliminates most of your work.

Most of the lightweight and modular track light components simply snap together. But you need to plan and measure carefully to know how many of each kind of component you'll need to accomplish the effect you want.

The electrified tracks themselves come in two-, four-, and eight-foot sections that can be plugged together end to end to make a continuous track of almost any length. If you want to turn a corner or run a track all the way around the room's ceiling, there are T-, X-, and L-couplings that automatically change the track's direction of travel. Two- and three-circuit components also are available, so that you can wire in separate switches to control different lights at any point along the track.

If the room already has a switch-controlled ceiling fixture you probably can remove it and substitute a track-light power junction at that point. Most tracks can be fed power from one end, at a coupling, or—in some cases—at any point in between. If there is no ceiling fixture box, you'll have to install one as explained on pages 146 and 147.

Computing power loads

One thing to keep in mind is that multiple-light track systems can demand a great deal of power, depending upon how many fixtures you intend to install. Where the original ceiling fixture may have been supplying power to a single 75- or 100-watt light bulb, it may now have to feed six or eight bulbs of the same size.

Can the circuit handle that demand? If not, you're going to blow a fuse or trip a circuit breaker at the service panel when you activate the lights. Circuits are rated at the service panel in terms of amps. Ceiling fixtures and wall outlets are typically fed by 15-amp circuits.

To find out if the circuit can take the new load, add up the wattage of each fixture. Using the formula amps equals watts divided by volts, you can figure the amperage requirements of each device on a particular circuit. For example, six track lights, each with 100-watt bulbs, equals a total demand of 600 watts. Divided by 120 volts (typical for most circuits) this yields a power pull of five amps. That sounds as if you have 10 amps to spare, but remember that single circuit may provide power to fixtures and receptacles in other rooms. So be sure to add in the amperage demand from other sources on the same line. Could the circuit take it if they all demanded service at the same time? If not, you may have to add a new circuit or distribute the electrical burden among other circuits.

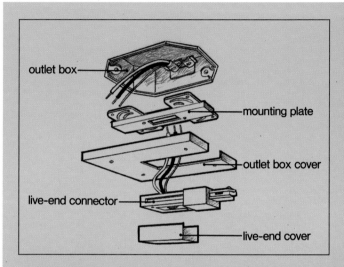

outlet box

mounting plate

outlet box cover

live-end connector

live-end cover

1 A track lighting system begins with a single ceiling box feeding power to a track, not to each fixture. With the power off, mount a connector—a live-end type, as shown, or a center feed—to the box. A special mounting plate attaches to the outlet box. A cover conceals the box and holds the connector.

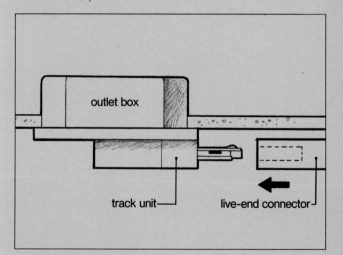

outlet box

track unit

live-end connector

4 The hard part is over. From here on out, it's just a matter of snapping the track lighting modules together. Add the first piece of track to the live-end connector you've already installed. You simply insert the track's leads into the live end's female coupling. Then push the track up against the ceiling clips.

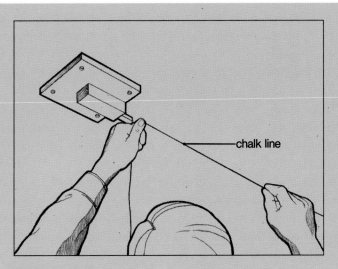

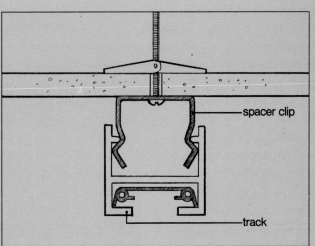

2 Next, make an on-the-ceiling map by snapping a chalk line from the connector's center along the route you want the track to follow. Each end of the line should be the same distance from the wall. If you don't have a chalk line, use a long, straight board and chart your course with a pencil.

chalk line

3 Spacer clips attached to the ceiling hold the track in place as shown here. Following the chalk lines, hold a spacer clip against the ceiling, then mark and drill the holes for toggle bolts. Space the clips at even intervals. You'll need at least two clips for each length of 2- and 4-foot track, three for 8-footers.

spacer clip

track

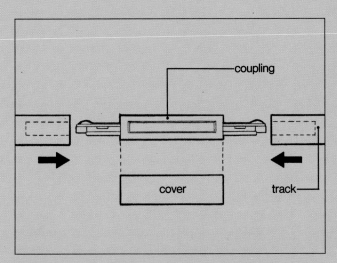

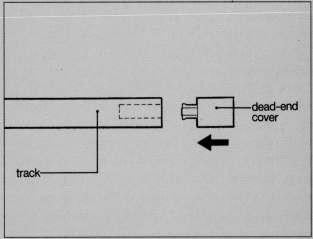

coupling

cover

track

track

dead-end cover

5 To expand the system, add a coupling to join two or more lengths of track together. Push the couplings and track ends together as you go. Special snap-on covers will camouflage the joints. Each manufacturer's track lighting components differ somewhat, so don't count on interchanging them.

6 When you've gone as far as you want to go with a single length of track, add a dead-end cover as a finishing touch. If you want to change directions, add a T-, X-, or L-coupling. After you've installed all the tracks, you can clip on lights anywhere you want, and move them any time you like.

INSTALLING A
LUMINOUS CEILING

If you're looking for a way to bathe a dim room with even, glare-free light, consider topping it off with a luminous ceiling. Translucent plastic panels directly below fluorescent lights camouflage the fixtures and distribute uniform illumination throughout the room. In between the series of fluorescent lights are acoustic ceiling panels.

Ideally suited to workshops, garages, and basements, a luminous ceiling can be installed anywhere there's adequate headroom. To check out the space you have in mind, measure from the floor to the existing ceiling or joists overhead. You need a minimum height of eight feet. Accounting for the thickness of the fixtures and about three inches of clear space under them (so you can fit panels into place), a suspended ceiling will drop headroom to 7½ feet, the legal minimum in most communities.

The components for suspended ceilings, available at most home centers, make installation a relatively easy job. You simply attach lightweight aluminum or steel channels to the walls and suspend them from ceiling joists with wire and screw eyes. Ceiling panels—opaque acoustical material and the plastic diffusers—lie atop the channels. The drawings at right take you through a typical installation.

Choosing fixtures

If energy efficiency is important to you, you should know that there are two kinds of fluorescent fixtures: those classified as rapid-start and those classified as delayed-start. A delayed-start fixture uses less electricity than a rapid-start type because it has a "starter" that preheats the cathodes inside the tubes. Delayed-start fixtures won't light up quite as

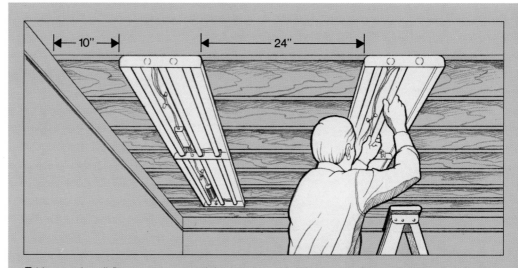

1 You can install fluorescent lights directly above a suspended ceiling with special brackets that attach to the cross tees. But attaching them directly to the joists above is probably easier and, because you won't need the brackets, slightly less costly.

Knock-out disks in the ends of the fixtures allow you to wire a series of fluorescent lights together so that one switch can control them all. Just remove the knock-outs before you put up the lights. Then, use hefty wood screws to attach the fixture housings end-to-end across the joists. Space rows of fluorescent fixtures about 24 inches apart and about 10 inches from the walls.

4 Following a chalk line that makes allowances for appropriate clearances above and below the new ceiling, attach wall angles around the perimeter of the room, aligning their bottom edges with the chalk line.

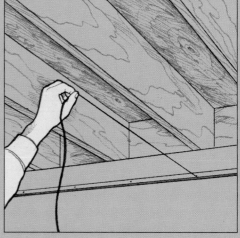

5 Next, stretch taut, level string lines across the room at several points. These will serve as guides to help you hang the cross tees that will support the lay-in acoustic ceiling panels and light-diffuser panels.

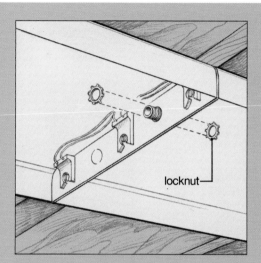

2 To tie two or more fluorescent fixtures together end to end (or even side to side), install threaded nipple couplings through the knockouts. These increase stability and make wiring a snap.

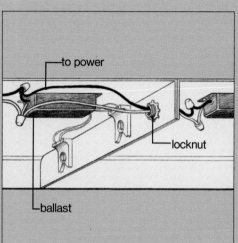

3 Finally, connect the lights to each other—using jumper wires and plastic wire nuts—and then to a switch-controlled ceiling box. Now you can install the suspended ceiling grid itself.

6 Starting a border tile's distance from the wall, drive screw eyes into every other joist. Hang and twist wire. Repeat at four-foot intervals. Loop wire through holes in main tees, level tees, and twist wire tight.

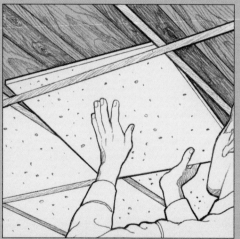

7 To complete the grid, use a sharp knife to install cross tees between the main tees. Trim and fit border panels. Fill in the rest of the grid with uncut panels. Under the lights, install clear, translucent, or egg-crate diffusers.

fast as the rapid-start tubes, but the difference is usually just a few seconds.

If you want to further improve the amount and quality of light from a luminous ceiling installation, cover the surfaces above the new ceiling with two coats of flat white paint.

Dimmers for fluorescents
Dimmers that can control one to eight fluorescent fixtures are installed the same way as incandescent dimmers. But you'll have to equip each of the fixtures with a special ballast, a device that sends current to the cathodes at each end of the tube. Dimming ballasts currently are available only for 4-foot-long, 40-watt, rapid-start lamps.

Before you disconnect the original ballast, make a diagram that shows which wires go where. Wire the replacement ballast the same way. Install the fixture or fixtures, then wire the dimmer switch according to package directions (or see pages 150 and 151), and restore power.

As an alternative to the trouble and expense of installing fluorescent dimmers, consider controlling a luminous ceiling system with two or more conventional toggle switches wired to turn on different fixtures.

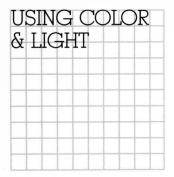

WHERE TO GO FOR MORE INFORMATION

Better Homes and Gardens® Books

Would you like to learn more about using color and light in your home? These Better Homes and Gardens® books can help.

Better Homes and Gardens®
NEW DECORATING BOOK
How to translate ideas into workable solutions for every room in your home. Choosing a style, furniture arrangements, windows, walls and ceilings, floors, lighting, and accessories. 433 color photos, 76 how-to illustrations, 432 pages.

Better Homes and Gardens®
DOLLAR-STRETCHING DECORATING
An excellent source for ideas and projects that make your dollar work harder. Shows how to use imagination, ingenuity, and know-how to sidestep high costs while stepping up style, comfort, and quality. Filled with easy-to-accomplish ideas, practical suggestions, do-it-yourself projects, and how-to drawings. 192 pages.

Better Homes and Gardens®
COMPLETE GUIDE TO HOME REPAIR,
MAINTENANCE, AND IMPROVEMENT
Inside your home, outside your home, your home's systems, basics you should know. Anatomy and step-by-step drawings illustrate components, tools, techniques, and finishes.
515 how-to techniques; 75 charts; 2,734 illustrations; 552 pages.

Better Homes and Gardens®
COMPLETE GUIDE TO GARDENING
A comprehensive guide for beginners and experienced gardeners. Houseplants, lawns and landscaping, trees and shrubs, greenhouses, insects and diseases. 461 color photos, 434 how-to illustrations, 37 charts, 552 pages.

Better Homes and Gardens®
DO-IT-YOURSELF HOME REPAIRS
How-to illustrations help you make carpentry, cabinetry, wiring, plumbing, and household repairs and improvements. Projects range from replacing a worn lamp cord to building new kitchen cabinets. More than 803 drawings, 14 charts, 320 pages.

Better Homes and Gardens®
LIVING THE COUNTRY LIFE
This beautiful book illustrates how city dwellers and suburbanites, as well as rural folks, have incorporated the country look into their homes. There are special sections on country furniture, floor coverings, window and wall treatments, crafts and collectibles, and more. 291 color photos, 80 black-and-white photos, 320 pages.

Better Homes and Gardens®
STEP-BY-STEP BASIC WIRING
Getting to know your system, solving electrical problems, making electrical improvements, electrical basics and procedures. 22 projects, 286 illustrations, 96 pages.

Other Sources of Information

Many professional and special-interest associations publish catalogs, style books, or product brochures that are available upon request.

American Society of Interior Designers (ASID)
730 Fifth Avenue
New York, NY 10019

American Furniture Manufacturers Association
P.O. Box HP-7
High Point, NC 27261

American Home Lighting Institute
435 North Michigan Avenue
Chicago, IL 60611

Carpet and Rug Institute
P.O. Box 2048
Dalton, GA 30720

General Electric
Nela Park
Cleveland, OH 44112
(800) 626-2000

National Association of Furniture Manufacturers
8401 Connecticut Avenue, Suite 911
Washington, DC 20015

ACKNOWLEDGMENTS

Architects and Designers

The following is a page-by-page listing of the interior designers, architects, and project designers whose works appear in this book.

Cover
 Rita Hooker
Pages 6-7
 Rogers Unlimited
Pages 8-9
 Philip Young;
 Jeffrey Walker and Sam
 Yazzolino
Pages 10-11
 Elaine Becker
Pages 12-13
 David A. De Angelis, Picture
 House
Pages 14-15
 Peter Scantlebury
 and Don Anderson,
 Color Design Art
Pages 16-17
 Ben Lloyd
Page 18
 Richar Johnnson
Page 19
 Bob Barrett
Pages 20-21
 Ron W. Sorenson, ASID
Pages 22-23
 Sharon Schnackenberg;
 Himmel Bonner Architects
Pages 28-29
 Rita Hooker
Page 38
 George Pappageorge and
 David Haymes
Page 39
 Morley Smith
Pages 40-41
 Cal Lewis
Pages 42-43
 Lee Bayard
Pages 44-45
 Inez Saunders, Inez
 Saunders and Associates,
 Inc.; James Dwinell, A.I.A.
Pages 46-47
 Lyle Skinner
Pages 48-49
 Interdesign, Inc.; Juline Beier

Pages 50-51
 James R. Ruddock
Pages 52-53
 Caroline Murray
Pages 54-55
 W.E. Johnson
Pages 56-57
 Susan Connelly
Pages 58-59
 Alexandra Rico
Pages 60-61
 Bloodgood Architects
Pages 62-63
 Carol Siegmeister, Taylor/
 Seigmeister Associates
Pages 64-65
 Bryan Shiffler, AIA
Pages 66-67
 Robert A.M. Stern
Pages 68-69
 Beverly Balk Interiors;
 Anthony Marano
Pages 70-71
 Barrett/Siskin
Pages 72-73
 Donna Warner and
 Karen Williams
Pages 74-75
 James McQuiston,
 Archonics
Pages 76-77
 Stephen Wadsworth and
 Vincas Meilus, Meilus and
 Wadsworth Architects
Pages 78-79
 R.I. Engel and Company;
 Kailer Grant
Pages 80-81
 Himmel Bonner Architects
Pages 82-83
 Pat Moitra, Burger/Coplans

Pages 84-87
 Kenneth Nadler, AIA
Pages 88-91
 Ron W. Sorenson, ASID
Pages 92-93
 Keith Gasser, Jesse
 Benesch & Associates
Pages 94-95
 Gallery Five Interiors;
 Anthony Marano
Page 97
 Jerome Brown & Associates
Pages 98-99
 Bloodgood Architects;
 Nancy Jansson
Pages 100-101
 Stephen Mead Associates;
 Ron W. Sorenson, A.S.I.D.
Pages 102-103
 Thomas Boccia; Rogers
 Unlimited, Inc.
Pages 104-105
 Jeffrey and Sally Miller/Rust,
 Orling, and Neale; Himmell
 Bonner Architects
Page 106
 Thomas L. Thomson, AIA
Pages 122-123
 Stephen Lloyd and William
 Grover of Moore, Grover
 Harper, PC
Pages 126-127
 Charles High Crain, AIA; Bo
 and Thornton, Stanley
 Goldstein
Pages 130-131
 James McQuiston,
 Archonics
Pages 132-133
 Jon Cockrell; Linda Joan
 Smith
Pages 134-135
 Thomas Boccia
Pages 136-137
 Thomas Boccia;
 Nancy Elliott

Photographers and Illustrators

We extend our thanks to the following photographers and illustrators, whose creative talents and technical skills contributed much to this book.

Peter Aaron/ESTO
Ernest Braun
Ross Chappel
de Gennaro Studios
Lisl Dennis
Harry Hartman
Hedrich-Blessing
Thomas Hooper
Hopkins Associates
Fred Lyon
Maris/Semel
Norman McGrath
Chris Mead
Carson Ode
Mitchel Osborne
John Rogers
Joseph Standart
John Vaughan
Peter Vitale
Jessie Walker

Manufacturers and Associations

Our appreciation goes to the following manufacturers and companies who contributed to this book.

Advanced Lighting
Albright Lighting and Interiors
General Electric
Halo Lighting, a division of
 McGraw-Edison
Lamplighter
Thomas Industries
Winnie Williams Designs

INDEX

Page numbers in *italics* refer to photographs or illustrated text.

Have BETTER HOMES
AND GARDENS® magazine
delivered to your door.
For information, write to:
MR. ROBERT AUSTIN
P.O. BOX 4536
DES MOINES, IA 50336